Word by Word

"As a cradle Catholic who has at times taken our beautiful prayers for granted, *Word by Word* caused me to stop, think, and really reflect on who our Blessed Mother is and the important role she plays in bringing us and keeping us close to Jesus."

Teresa Tomeo
EWTN host and bestselling author of *Extreme Makeover*

"Sarah Reinhard has—like the Woman Wisdom in Proverbs 8—laid a great feast for us by assembling some of the best Catholic writers of our time to squeeze the juice out of one of the richest prayers ever to emerge from the Catholic tradition, the Hail Mary. Drink up!"

Mark P. Shea
Author of *Mary, Mother of the Son*

"I find *Word by Word* absolutely fascinating and delightful in both form and substance. This book is worth far more than you will pay for it."

Daniel Burke
Executive Director of the *National Catholic Register*

"Real men know in their hearts that the Hail Mary is the perfect prayer. What better way to pray than to use the words of an angel to ask for the help of the Mother of God—to ask for our Mother's help. Thank you, Sarah, for inviting us to slow down and cherish every word of this heart song to Mary. A wonderful book!"

David and Valerie Calvillo
Founders of Real Men Pray the Rosary

"With *Word by Word*, we are invited to step inside the simple words and really think them through. These meditations remind us that an engagement with the Mother of God is full of both grace and power, and that our every thirteen-second supplication is a boomlet toward heaven, for the sake of the world."

Elizabeth Scalia
Catholic blogger and author of *Strange Gods*

"Sarah Reinhard has infused our most common prayer with the spirit of the ancient Sabbath—giving the Hail Mary the leisurely, loving reading and recitation it deserves. How appropriate that we should come to pray with the peaceful, contemplative spirit Mary brought to the Holy Family."

Mike Aquilina
EWTN host, writer, author, and speaker

"This book is a gem for all who seek friendship with God in the prayer of the Rosary. The message: slow down and allow the richness and variety of God's abundant grace in daily life to come alive in your praying heart."

Rev. Wilfred Raymond, C.S.C.
President of Holy Cross Family Ministries

"Sarah Reinhard and her colleagues have found a simple, approachable, and potentially life-changing method for bringing the gorgeous, scriptural Hail Mary to vibrant new life. You'll never pray a Rosary the same way again."

Greg Willits
Founder of *RosaryArmy.com*
Executive Director of Evangelization and Family Life Ministries
Archdiocese of Denver

"This little book will help you appreciate the Hail Mary in a deeper way and make the praying of your next Rosary that much more meaningful!"

Rev. Donald Calloway, M.I.C.
Author of *Under the Mantle*

"Such a simple concept written so beautifully well. Slow down, read a few pages, and find yourself pulled into a closer and more authentic relationship with Mary the Mother of God."

Danielle Bean
Publisher of *Catholic Digest*
Coauthor of *Small Steps for Catholic Moms*

"This is a wonderful book, prayer guide, homage to the Blessed Mother, and a gift I plan to give all of my friends this year. Well done, Sarah Reinhard!"

Randy Hain
Author of *Journey to Heaven*
Cofounder of the *Integrated Catholic Life*

"Reading *Word by Word* is like participating in a warm, honest, faith-sharing session among good friends. A marvelous way to enter into more intimate communion with the Blessed Mother, which means, ultimately, gazing more deeply into the face of her Son."

Amy Welborn
Author of *Wish You Were Here*

Word by Word

SLOWING

DOWN

WITH THE

HAIL MARY

Edited by

SARAH A.
REINHARD

AVE MARIA PRESS AVE Notre Dame, Indiana

© 2015 by Sarah A. Reinhard

Founded in 1865, Ave Maria Press is a ministry of the United States Province of Holy Cross.

www.avemariapress.com

Paperback: ISBN-13 978-1-59471-640-9

E-book: ISBN-13 978-1-59471-641-6

Cover image "Hail Mary" © Jen Norton, JenNortonArtStudio.com.

Cover design by Katherine Ross.

Text design by John R. Carson.

Printed and bound in the United States of America.

Library of Congress Cataloging-in-Publication Data
Word by word : slowing down with the Hail Mary / edited by Sarah A. Reinhard.
    pages cm
  ISBN 978-1-59471-640-9 -- ISBN 1-59471-640-4
  1. Ave Maria. I. Reinhard, Sarah, editor.
  BX2175.A8W67 2015
  242'.74--dc23
                        2015021925

Hail Mary, full of grace.

The Lord is with thee.

Blessed art thou among women,

and blessed is the fruit of thy womb, Jesus.

Holy Mary, Mother of God,

pray for us sinners,

now and at the hour of our death.

Amen.

Contents

Thank you to those who made this project possible,
including, but not limited to:
the contributors,
my readers and supporters,
the excellent team at Ave Maria Press,
my family,
and my best friend and spouse, Bob.

Introduction

I learned the Hail Mary sitting on a mattress on the floor, in the upstairs room of the last apartment I lived in before I got married. I was newly Catholic and I had a special intention. I was convinced the Blessed Mother was the right one to approach.

As I stumbled through the Rosary that first time, without the benefit of the audio aids that would later help me to "get it," I didn't get a shock of understanding. The lights didn't flicker. Nothing exploded in a shower of sparks.

But I kept plugging along, struggling. The Rosary became my companion on commutes, and I discovered a CD that helped me learn the words. I would keep a rosary in my purse, but I learned how to check it off on my fingers when I didn't have or couldn't use a rosary. Time passed and that intention was updated with something else. Then I put the Rosary away for a while, only to pick it up again.

Now that I've had the Rosary as my companion for years, I notice that when I'm troubled, when I can't find the words, or when I am fearful, I latch on to the Hail Mary. Does saying it just occupy the part of my mind that needs activity? Possibly. But I think there's more to it.

A few years ago, I woke in the middle of the night. I was on a trip without my husband, and the baby and toddler were both snoring beauties. Nothing was amiss except that there was an urge so strong it was almost as if someone were *telling* me to pray for my safety.

I don't know how long I lay there, terrified. All I could pray was a litany of Hail Marys. It was the only thing that came out. I had never had an experience where a memorized prayer was a way of praying past the fear completely clouding my mind except in my dreams.

I don't often have nightmares, except when I'm pregnant. Then they are no-holds-barred adventures. During one of my pregnancies, I remember feeling petrified and waking myself up by praying Hail Marys. You might say it's become my blankie prayer.

Just as my children cling to their worn-soft, faded blankies, so I cling to my Blessed Mother's skirt through this prayer. When my heart aches, I cry out a Hail Mary. When I need to be held in my sorrow, it's a Hail Mary that comes out. When I'm worried or troubled, the words I can't find on my own shape up as a Hail Mary.

I wrap my babies in soft blankets, bundling them against hurt, and God has wrapped me in the blankie prayer that I've become as comfortable with as the old quilt from my childhood, the one on my bed. I hold my children after they fall and put bandages on their scrapes, just as God wraps his arms around me through the love of his mother, which I'm always reminded of when I say a Hail Mary.

I pray it unconsciously, the way my children grab my hand without even knowing it when we're walking side by side. It's a comfort to me, and I'm so blessed to have it. When I don't have words for the desires of my heart, I always have the Hail Mary. When I'm lonely or sad or just at odds with the world, I have the Hail Mary. In the Hail Mary, I find so very many spiritual delights, not the least of which is how it leads me, irrevocably, closer to Mary's Son.

In 2011, Jennifer Fulwiler introduced me to a new way of looking at prayer: one word at a time. She hosted many guest writers at her blog, *Conversion Diary*, and they traveled through the Our Father one word at a time. It was a way of praying I had never considered and one that has stuck with me in the years since.

Of course, I couldn't resist considering my favorite prayer in light of this word-by-word approach. What would it be like to pray the Hail Mary deliberately, carefully weighing the importance and significance of every one of the forty-two words?

The book you hold in your hands represents the answer to that question. I approached a number of my favorite writers and friends, expecting a flurry of negative responses. What I received, instead, was the grace of seeing people put Mary's yes to work in the most beautiful way, by deliberately walking through the Hail Mary one word at a time.

The experience of praying this, my "blankie prayer," in such a slow and deliberate manner has sown many seeds in my spiritual life. I don't naturally do things slowly. I'm a process gal with an eye toward productivity: there's a lot on my list and the day is burning along. But when I stop and take a breath, praying in this intentional way, I find a different kind of comfort.

It's just as enriching as when I lean into the unconscious softness of it, turning to it without even considering what the words mean. My intellect gets engaged, and suddenly I notice different things. There's a new message for me each time I approach the Hail Mary slowly. A calmness is cultivated that forces me to live in the present moment in a way so few things in my modern life of gadgets and responsibilities require.

Though I'm no master at lectio divina, the sacred reading of scripture and praying along with it, I can't help but feel that's the same sort of thing we're doing here, praying the Hail Mary deliberately like this. We're slowing ourselves, focusing on each element.

And since the Hail Mary is based on scripture, that's not such a far-fetched way of approaching this prayer, is it?

Each element is important. Skip a *the* or an *of* and you can change the entire meaning of the sentence. Leave out a verb or a noun, and nothing makes sense.

So here we are. We'll take a journey together through the Hail Mary, word by word. The prayer will expand as we work our way from *Hail* to *Amen*. You may find yourself uncomfortable, inspired, confused, or even overwhelmed. Embrace that experience and let Mary guide you to her Son through it.

I am glad you're with us. I pray you'll join us in turning to Jesus through the intercession of his dear and beloved mother.

Hail Mary, full of grace

Fr. Patrick Toner

We all recognize the greeting of Gabriel. The Greek word *chairo* can be translated as "greeting," or "hail," or "rejoice." We commonly use greetings with multiple meanings, such as "Good morning." It can be a fact or a wish, and often it is meant to be both.

If Gabriel had greeted Mary in Hebrew, it would likely have been *shalom*, or "Peace be with you." The gospel was written in Greek, so the term *chairo* was used. The translation "Hail" speaks of saluting one of great favor. The Roman greeting "Hail Caesar" easily comes to mind. Certainly Gabriel understood whom he was greeting and the significance of the words that would follow.

In Nazareth, over the grotto of the Annunciation, there is a depiction of Mary and Gabriel overshadowed by the Holy Spirit. They are dancing with great joy. I love to consider what would make an angel dance. Gabriel was in the presence of a rare person, one totally filled with God's grace. His greeting must have been more akin to "Rejoice" than just a simple greeting.

Each time we pray "Hail Mary," we should welcome her into our hearts so that we may meditate on the mysteries with her. To greet her is to acknowledge that she is present to us. May that be a heartfelt and warm welcome, full of joy.

Prayer

How can you welcome Mary into your heart today? As you go throughout your day, pause at least once to pray the Hail Mary. As you're praying it, greet her and greet God through her presence in you.

Fr. Patrick Toner, a priest of forty years in the Diocese of Columbus, Ohio, has served as a pastor, military chaplain, prison chaplain, spiritual director, and editorialist.

Hail *Mary*, full of grace

❧

Deacon Tom Fox

What first came to mind when I thought of writing about the name Mary is related to my Irish heritage. I thought of the patriotic songwriter George M. Cohan, who wrote a song that has these words:

> For it is Mary, Mary
> Plain as any name can be . . .
> And there is something there that sounds so square
> It's a grand old name
> Yes—Mary is a grand old name.

I seem to remember my mother—whose name, coincidentally, was Mary—playing that song on our basement piano while Dad played the fiddle.

I discovered the hymn "Mary the Dawn" during my first year as a deacon candidate when we purchased our Liturgy of the Hours books. I had never heard of "Mary the Dawn" before then. In just fourteen lines, I found a sensitive theology for ordinary folks that beautifully and tenderly describes the

Incarnation and the intimacy between Mother and Son. All but lost in history, these words were likely a poem about Mary and the totally unique relationship that exists between the Tabernacle and the God-Son reposed in her.

Mary the Dawn

Mary the dawn, Christ the Perfect Day;
Mary the gate, Christ the Heavenly Way!
Mary the root and Christ the Mystic Vine;
Mary the grape and Christ the Sacred Wine!
Mary the wheat, Christ the Living Bread;
Mary the stem, Christ the Rose blood-red!
Mary the font, Christ the Cleansing Flood;
Mary the cup, Christ the Saving Blood!
Mary the temple, Christ the temple's Lord;
Mary the shrine, Christ the God adored!
Mary the beacon, Christ the Haven's Rest,
Mary the mirror, Christ the Vision Blest.
Mary the mother, Christ the mother's son
By all things blest, while endless ages run.
Amen.

If you are a devotee of Mary, you are aware that there are many titles for our Blessed Mother. There is no person from our Christian scripture and heritage who has been so honored as to the quantity or the scope of the titles as our Mother Mary. I have compiled a nonexhaustive list of these titles for use in meditation, which can be found in the appendix.

Prayer

We often give nicknames to those we love. Choose one of the titles or nicknames of Mary and use it in place of her name when you pray the Hail Mary today. If you need ideas for a title, see the appendix.

Deacon Tom Fox is the cofounder of the Catholic Vitamins *podcast.*

Hail Mary, *full* of grace

Jaymie Stuart Wolfe

Full. *Full of yourself. Full of baloney. Full of it.* There are instances in which full really means empty. It's so easy to chase our appetites, to fill ourselves with what we think will satisfy our hunger. But that is precisely how we end up empty.

Full of life. Full of hope. A full heart. These are things we cannot acquire ourselves, things we must receive. To be full, we must have *been filled*.

We may look to others as well as to our own ingenuity, but there is only One who can fill us. This is the very human truth that Mary knew and lived. God alone can fill the hungry with good things (Lk 1:53).

We live in a world of image and appearance where what we seem has become more important than what we are. All around us exquisitely crafted empty bottles are being sold as full ones. That's not difficult when no one is willing to take the stopper out and turn the bottle upside down. *Not one drop.* But, afraid we might miss out, a whole lot of us are quick to pay the price—one that's way too high for a pretty jar with nothing in it, one that none of us can really afford.

Sometimes "full" looks like less than empty. A positive pregnancy test. A negative MRI. A teenage girl from a backwater town in an unimportant province at the edge of the empire. A Virgin.

Mary is the human face of all that is full. She is filled with the unspoken hopes, the inspirations and dreams, the unknown longings of every human soul. Even before she conceives the Son of God, Mary is full of him. She has been his bondservant from the beginning. Mary is the culmination of human history, the sum of all of us, the hinge by which the door to salvation opens.

Across history and language, culture and race, flooding over every barrier we suffer and those we have devised, Mary's fullness overflows to us. She does not keep it for herself. "When the fullness of time had come, God sent his Son, born of a woman" (Gal 4:4). For Mary, now is the fullness of time; today is the day to birth salvation into the world and place him into our hands. Full.

Prayer

How are you full today? What in your life feels too full or not full enough? Pray the Hail Mary and consider the fullness God wants for you. Take a full breath as you pray it and let go of the pressures you feel to fill whatever is empty. Leave that to God.

Jaymie Stuart Wolfe, a wife, mother of eight, and Catholic convert, echoes God's universal call to holiness through her work as an author, columnist, speaker, musician, and full-time editor at Pauline Books & Media.

Hail Mary, full of grace

Carol Ann Chybowski

This humble little breath of air carries tremendous power, so much power that Merriam-Webster's online dictionary lists no less than twelve distinct definitions. *Of* denotes origin, as when we say someone lives north of the tracks or is born of a line of kings. *Of* denotes the basic component of an object, as when we say that a cup is made of gold. But most often *of* is a word that defines belonging and relationship. We are the sons and daughters *of* God.

In the Hail Mary, *of* carries all three elements: origin, composition, and relationship. It looks behind itself to Mary. We are speaking about Mary and her relationship with God. She is full, filled by God in the best sense. But what is it that Mary is full of if not God himself? Mary is of God. She belongs to him.

Of looks ahead to grace. Mary is full of grace. Grace is the basic fiber of her being. Because of this little word *of*, we know that she belongs to grace, and grace belongs to her. Mary is the Mother of God. She belongs to God, and God belongs to her—he is her own Son. Mary is the Mother of the Church. She belongs to the Church, even as we ourselves do.

As you pray, ask yourself: What am I of? Where do I come from? And to whom do I belong?

Prayer

The Holy Spirit is like a breath, like the wind, like a still, small voice. Find a breath of silence today and pray the Hail Mary, focusing on your breathing as you do so. With each breath, open yourself to the small—but significant—things the Holy Spirit has in store for you today.

Carol Ann Chybowski is a longtime member of the Catholic Writers Guild whose work has appeared in two volumes: A Community of Voices: An Anthology of Santa Barbara *and* Spiritual Awakenings: Stories of Praise and Redemption.

Hail Mary, full of *grace*

❧

Kate Wicker

I once was talking to my ninety-year-old nana about my special devotion to Our Blessed Mother. Nana, the faith superstar and über-Catholic matriarch of our family, surprised me by saying it took her a long time to develop a relationship with Mary. "When I was having a hard day [raising nine kids], I'd sometimes find myself thinking, 'Mary didn't have it so bad. She had one perfect child.'"

I get what my nana was saying. Not only did Mary give birth to God himself, but also she was full of grace. As in perfect herself. Sometimes it's hard to feel like I'll ever measure up to Mary's beauty, piety, and sheer awesomeness when I can't even keep up with laundry and have been known to lock myself in the bathroom to escape the madness rather than calmly diffuse the rioting natives.

Yet what I also find in Mary—aside from her being a mirror of perfection—is a willingness to embrace all her imperfect little children (including me) and to hold them close even when they're anything but full of grace.

Mary also helps to reveal what a beautiful thing God's grace is and remind us that it's there for our taking.

A friend once compared parenthood to running a marathon or an ultramarathon. Her husband has competed in both, and my friend admitted that she couldn't even begin to think about physically challenging herself to that degree. But her husband reminded her that he gets the same kind of response—"I could never do what you do and have so many children!"—from others who discover he has eight children. She wrote, "People are capable of doing difficult, unfathomable things." Mary is proof of this.

From the moment of the annunciation, she said yes to God over and over. She even said yes to watching her only child suffer and die. She achieved and endured unfathomable things. How did she do this? With God's grace.

I know I'm far from being full of grace. Mary was the first to receive this gift. The Mother of God is not someone I need to compete with or avoid—I'll always find myself coming up short. Rather, she is a beautiful reminder of what God has in mind for us all.

God called me to be a wife and mom. Every day he asks me to relinquish control, to bend to his will, to trust as Mary did even when I don't understand what's going on—like why my two-year-old keeps saying there's a button in her nose. Did she really shove a button up her nostril, or is she just trying to make me crazy? Will I answer his call? Will I accept that he wants nothing more than to bless me, to lavish me with grace, and to lead me in living a life of trust and surrender to him? Or will I instead just give up, believe that grace is not for a sinner such as I am, and hide behind a litany of can'ts?

We don't need to be immaculately conceived and rid ourselves of every sin and annoying quirk to experience a fulfilling, happy relationship with Christ. All we have to do is take his grace where we can get it by staying close to him, by welcoming him into our hearts and our homes at the dawn of each new day, and by begging our Mama—his Mama—to show us what it means to be led by grace.

"My grace is sufficient for you, for power is made perfect in weakness" (2 Cor 12:9). Indeed his grace is all we need, and the smallest drops of it can fill us up. But the first step to having grace means being open to receiving it. That grace may come in the form of a generous offer of a friend to take our kids for an hour so we can rest or go to adoration, or we may find the strength to make it through the witching hour after we receive a spontaneous hug from a child.

Wherever we find the grace—in our home, in our spouse, in our Bible, or in our hearts—let's be grateful for it and allow it to serve as a reminder that like Mary, the handmaid of the Lord, we're at our best not when we're questioning ourselves and what we have to offer but when we focus on what God can do through us.

Prayer

Grace is a gift, but sometimes it's a gift we don't want or think we need. Today, as you pray the Hail Mary, close your eyes. Imagine overflowing with grace. How might that feel? What might that look like? Whom might it have an effect on in your life?

Kate Wicker is a regular contributor to Catholic Digest *and the author of* Weightless: Making Peace with Your Body. *Find out more at KateWicker.com.*

The Lord is with thee

Mary C. Gildersleeve

The: made with two of the most frequently used letters in the English language (*e* and *t*) and the ninth most frequently used (*h*). *The*: a three-letter word that warrants only six points in the game of Scrabble. *The*: three common letters pregnant with meaning.

The word *the* is known as a definite article. An article means a word that combines with a noun to indicate the degree of definiteness (specificity) of the reference being made by the noun. For instance, an article indicating degree with a noun would be *a* toy, *an* apple, *some* families, *the* book.

The is the only article that carries with it definiteness, specificity. *The* is the only article that defines the noun as being the only one, a specific, unique example of the subject.

So *the* in the Hail Mary means that Mary has *the* God with her. She isn't surrounded by multiple gods or earthly lords. She isn't distracted by other gods or material beings.

She lives and loves in the small town of Nazareth in Galilee and yet she is beyond this little town. Mary's faith and life are placed solely and completely in God the Father, and his love is placed in her.

He is with her.

The one true God, the Lord of all, the Creator, is with the Blessed Mother, knowing of her faith and sanctity, imbuing her being with his love and care. There are no others to whom Mary turns; Mary turns only to God. She initially questions the archangel Gabriel's meaning but accepts the angel's words because she has faith in the one true God. And God knows this and entrusts her with his only begotten Son.

The one and only archangel Gabriel comes to the one and only Mary of Nazareth, betrothed to the one and only Joseph (a descendant of King David), to let her know that the one and only God, the true Lord, is with her, beside her, carrying her through. And she is full of grace!

That's a lot of meaning packed into those three little letters—*t-h-e*.

Prayer

Little things can make a big difference. We don't have to look far to see proof of this in our everyday lives. As you pray the Hail Mary today, think of one little thing you can offer God. Maybe you'll even have a chance to see the little thing blossom into a big difference!

Homeschooling mom, hand-knits designer, author, and librarian for a Catholic high school, Mary C. Gildersleeve keeps very busy and relies heavily on the Blessed Mother for lots of intercessory prayers. Find out more at MaryGildersleeve.com.

The *Lord* is with thee

Brandon Vogt

My third-grade basketball team had just one superstar, and his name was Deon. The rest of us were a goofy mix of driveway legends and playground wannabes, but Deon was the real deal. He had a Herculean 4'9" frame and skills honed on the notoriously rough courts of suburban Orlando.

With Deon at the helm, our whole season was a breeze. He led us in scoring each game as we collected win after win, sailing smoothly into the playoffs.

There things got a little more challenging. The first playoff game came down to the wire, yet Deon's late-game heroics produced a win. The next game was even tighter. But once again, channeling his inner Jordan, Deon willed us to victory.

But the third game was different. It was about five minutes before tip-off, and the whole team stood in a huddle. Everyone was quiet, even the coach. We exchanged nervous glances as we all noticed the same thing. Deon wasn't there.

We frantically called his house and asked around, yet nobody knew where he was. The ref walked with the ball toward midcourt and it was clear that Deon wouldn't make it. So the game started without him.

As expected, so did the onslaught. Within a couple of minutes we were down by double digits, and the first quarter ended along with our hopes. But then something happened. My memory gets a little hazy at this point, but here's how I remember it.

The gym doors slammed open, light poured in from all angles, and, accompanied by the glories of heaven, Deon sailed in on a cloud. He was back! Our star had risen! And we all breathed a sigh of relief. Everything would be okay.

Deon entered the game and poured in bucket after bucket. Our whole team was fired up and Deon was putting on a show. He first brought us within range, then tied the game, then gave us the lead. We eventually won and Deon was hailed by everyone for the miraculous comeback.

I can hear that same sigh of relief when the archangel Gabriel tells Mary, "The Lord is with you." To know that your hero is here, that your savior is by your side, and that everything will be okay is like hearing, "The cancer is gone" or "Daddy is here."

Imagine hearing that the Lord of the cosmos does not just love you from afar, is not just dabbling in human affairs, but is actually with you in the here and now.

The Lord who spun the planets and hung the stars.

The Lord who sings the earth into existence and breathes out life.

The Lord who saved Noah from the sea and brought Moses right through another.

The Lord of hosts, the Lord of the universe, the master of history.

That one—*that* Lord—is with you.

How shocking and comforting that must have been. Perhaps it was this greeting, this affirmation of God's companionship, that gave Mary the courage to deliver her great *fiat*, her "let it be done."

Because when the hero is here, all is well. And so it is for us.

Prayer

Does God, the Lord of the universe, really care about my small worries and concerns, the daily trivialities and silliness that often consumes me? When I look to Mary, I see that he does indeed. Pray the Hail Mary today and let yourself be hugged by the words; accept yourself as the beloved child you are.

Brandon Vogt is an author, blogger, and the content director at Fr. Robert Barron's Word on Fire Catholic ministries.

The Lord *is* with thee

Mark Szewczak

Mary, the mother-to-be of Jesus the Christ, is seen in a snapshot at the beginning of this prayer. She was a holy, righteous maiden of a poor Jewish family living in an out-of-the-way village.

In the first chapter of St. Luke's gospel the archangel Gabriel greeted her and she was troubled. Troubled? I suspect any of us would be terrified or seized with mind-numbing awe at the sight of a heaven-sent messenger! Was it the angelic apparition that caused her to be troubled? St. Luke tells us it was the greeting: "Hail, favored one! The Lord is with you."

The Lord *is* with you. A definite, abrupt, forceful statement that the Creator of the universe is with her, a poor Galilean girl. To her it was a *right now* moment. He is with her right now.

Putting ourselves in her sandals for a moment, how could we dare believe the concept that the Lord God of all creation, existing beyond time and space, all-powerful, all-knowing, is with us? Like Mary did, we live in a world that demands that we earn our bread, feed our children, and deal with the hardships and mundane repetitions of life. Did she ever before confront this incredible reality: God is with her? Have we? If we think of it, dare to believe it, what does it do in our souls? What did it do to her soul as she confronted the immense reality of God with her?

In those few moments with the angel she found the strength to say that most important yes. She knows she's not alone. God is with her. Her Son came to show the rest of us the same shocking, otherworldly truth. His coming was foretold in Isaiah, who called him Emmanuel, a name that means "God is with us."

God loves us each so completely that he *is* with each of us right now, always and everywhere. We needed Jesus to give us this message and to keep giving it. Two thousand years later we still have trouble comprehending.

May we remember, in our praying the Hail Mary, the peasant girl, now reigning in heaven, who was given the message, was troubled, but then said yes. May we also have the courage to say yes.

Prayer

Though we are often busy, we are not often active in the way the word *is* invites us to be. Today, let yourself be moved to action after you pray the Hail

Mary. What is God asking of us? How can we respond in the present tense, with the kind of yes that Mary shows us?

Mark Szewczak is a husband, father, and grandfather living in suburban Philadelphia. He is a candidate for the diaconate for the Archdiocese of Philadelphia.

The Lord is *with* thee

Nancy Carpentier Brown

"The Lord is with thee" was an interesting thing for the archangel Gabriel to say to Mary before she was the Mother of God, before she said yes to God.

We often hear the greeting in Mass, "The Lord be with you." It is a greeting of hope, one of calling. The priest or minister is praying over us, almost like a benediction, asking the Lord to come and be with us.

We have free will; we have a choice. We can let the Lord accompany us, be with us, or we can say no thank you, and God will leave us to our own defenses.

If we choose to, we respond, "And with your Spirit," asking the Lord to be with our minister, too. This closely follows what St. Paul prayed in Galatians: "The grace of our Lord Jesus Christ be with your spirit, brothers."

But for Mary, the angel doesn't take this tone of hopeful prayer. The angel is saying the Lord is with Mary.

With thee. With Mary. Accompanying Mary. The Spirit of the Lord is already in company with Mary, already in association with Mary, already connected with Mary—before the archangel Gabriel got there. That's because before the angel even got there, Mary had already been saying yes to God, had already asked the Lord to accompany her on her way. She'd always said yes. Church teaching tells us she never said no, not even once.

Two thousand years later when we pray these words, we do so with the knowledge that Mary is in heaven with God. There is no doubt about the saying, "The Lord is with you, Mary." Up in heaven, the Lord is with everyone. Everyone in heaven is in company with Jesus, God, and the Holy Spirit in that great Inn at the End of the World, taking part in the endless feast of the whole family of God.

May we say to God with all our hearts yes, yes, yes. Let it be said of us, "The Lord is with you." May our lives so shine forth God's presence that those around us can see that the Lord accompanies us on our earthly journey and so will be with us at our own final hour. Amen.

Prayer

The Lord is with us right now, at this very moment. Mary knows all about that: she has been with God in ways that we should aspire to. As you pray the Hail Mary today, ask for the grace to recognize God's presence in your life. Maybe even send a little "Hi" to him through the day when you see him!

Nancy Carpentier Brown works at the American Chesterton Society and is the author of Frances Chesterton's biography, The Woman Who Was Chesterton. *Find out more at MrsNancyBrown.blogspot.com.*

The Lord is with *thee*

❧ ❦ ❧

Jeff Young

"It ain't about me." I've been saying that for years. It doesn't mean I've always lived it. But I have said it.

We live in a me-focused society. We are trained all our lives, without being consciously aware of it, to be the center of our own universe. Even good people are infected with "me-itis." Even people striving to be holy.

Years ago, I was in the seminary. Twice. I spent two years in formation with the Missionaries of Charity Fathers, Mother Teresa's priests, in Tijuana, Mexico. Then, later (after a stint of bartending, believe it or not) I spent two more years in the seminary studying for the Diocese of Baton Rouge. I loved God as best as I could. I wanted to be holy. But, looking back, I can tell you that my "vocation" was all about me. I endured a long, confusing, and painful process before I came to know—in my bones, so to speak—that it is not about me.

My last year in the seminary I fell head over heels in love with the most beautiful woman in the world. Again. Yes, again.

She had been my best friend for a few years before I began studying for the Diocese of Baton Rouge, but we had drifted apart. Then an event took place my last year in the seminary that brought us back together: her younger brother died suddenly.

It's always tragic when a young person dies. Anthony was only twenty-one. It was his death that sparked lots of questions about faith and God in the heart of his sister. Since I had been her best friend, and since I was in the seminary (which means that I should know *something* about God, right?), she turned to me.

I did not expect to fall in love with her again. Falling in love was not part of my plan. You see, after years of drifting, years of trying to figure out who I was, I was finally there. I had purpose. I had direction. God was calling me to be a priest. Falling in love did not fit into that picture.

Yet, there I was. Helplessly in love. Feeling things I had never felt before. It made no sense to me. And as I tried to make sense of it all, as I tried to unravel what was happening to my heart, I suffered greatly. All this happened at the heart level. Deep stuff. Identity. All of a sudden, I found myself asking that question again, "Who am I?"

It's really difficult to put that experience into words. Over the years I have distilled the experience into a few expressions, a few ways to explain that time in my life. I've explained to people how, in retrospect, I seemed to be the one orchestrating "my vocation" to the priesthood. And that orchestration was exhausting. I was always on my toes, making sure I was playing the part right. I was always anxious. Thinking back now, I see that I desired the priesthood for me. It would validate my holiness. It would prove that God really did love me. It would prove that I was important.

Honestly, when I imagined what it would be like to be a priest, I imagined myself saying Mass or leading a eucharistic procession or benediction. Sometimes I imagined myself hearing confessions. But the day-to-day stuff that a priest does in the parish? I couldn't see myself doing that. Imagining the people I would serve as I priest? That never entered into my mind!

It wasn't until this young lady entered my life again that I started to think about somebody other than myself. God used her to show me that "it ain't about me." My healing from me-itis began with her.

All of a sudden, I was not in control. I was not orchestrating my vocation, and I was not orchestrating this newfound relationship either. God was. As my final year in the college seminary came to a close, I did not know what the future would hold. All I knew was that I had to take time off in order to see what this relationship was all about.

I graduated and got a job. A year and a half later I married my best friend, Char. I did not know what love was until she entered my life. Through Char I discovered that the most important question is not "Who am I?" but "Who are you?"

The family has been called the "school of love." It is in the family that we learn to love. It was before the altar in the beautiful gothic church of St. Patrick's in New Orleans in November 1998 that I began work on the only degree worth obtaining: love.

Love always focuses on the other, whether that other is God, or spouse, or children, or friends and family, or even strangers. When others are the focus, we are free. Free from me-itis. And free to love.

The angel assured Mary at the annunciation that the Lord was with her. Mary was not focused on herself. She was focused on the Lord, and so she was free to say yes. The world has not been the same ever since.

Mother Mary, help all of us to keep our eyes fixed on Jesus. Help us all (single, married, widowed, young, old) to say yes to the Lord like you did, so that one day we will graduate with honors from the school of love in this life and wake up rejoicing in the freedom of love in the next. Amen.

Prayer

Who is the "other" who needs your love today? How can you share that love through your words, actions, or prayers? Pray the Hail Mary today and let it be the doorway to that other who needs your love.

Jeff Young, founder, producer, and talent of The Catholic Foodie, *offers Catholic culinary inspiration to help families grow in faith around the table. Find out more at CatholicFoodie.com.*

Blessed art thou among women

Maria Morera Johnson

I treat myself to a burrito at a local fast-food joint about once a week. I can't exactly call it a highlight of my week, but the burrito gets the job done.

The early afternoon lunch run through the drive-through is efficient. Quick. Impersonal. Just the way I like it. Enter Gloria, the superfast, superaccurate cashier. She always tells me to "have a blessed day" when she hands me my order. Every single time. I've probably heard that about two hundred times since I started eating there, and I never gave it a thought until now.

What exactly is she saying? Is she blessing me? Is she blessing the day? Does it really matter? Yes. It matters a lot. A blessing is something special, and to be blessed, as Webster tells us, is to be hallowed, worthy of blessing, heavenly, holy. Beatified. Joyful. I particularly like that last one, joyful.

This eleventh word in the Hail Mary comes at a very important part. Following the greeting by the archangel Gabriel, "Hail Mary," we continue with "blessed art thou among women"—joyful among women. I always knew she was holy, but did not consider that she was full of joy at the thought of being the Mother of God. Of course she would be joyful.

This realization of the joy that accompanies the blessedness inspired me to read chapter 1 of Luke. In it, I was reminded of the events surrounding this astonishing news of the annunciation. First, Zechariah is assured of joy and gladness in Elizabeth's pregnancy. Then, Mary learns that she will conceive a Son, and she gives her yes to God. And then . . . Mary visits Elizabeth, and the child in Elizabeth's womb leaps for joy upon hearing her greeting. How did I miss this before?

Elizabeth tells Mary, "Most blessed are you among women" (Lk 1:42) and then again tells her, "Blessed are you who believed that what was spoken to you by the Lord would be fulfilled" (v. 45).

That is followed by the Canticle of Mary, the Magnificat, where Mary proclaims, "My soul proclaims the greatness of the Lord; my spirit rejoices in God my savior. For he has looked upon his handmaid's lowliness; behold, from now on will all ages call me blessed" (vv. 46–55).

There is a great deal of rejoicing going on! And how blessed are we that Mary said yes to it all. The *Catechism of the Catholic Church* explains how this act of faith is the root of this blessing: "The Virgin Mary most perfectly embodies the obedience of faith. By faith Mary welcomes the tidings and promise brought by the archangel Gabriel, believing that 'with God nothing will be impossible' and so giving her assent: 'Behold I am the handmaid of the Lord; let it be [done] to me according to your word.' . . . It is for this faith that all generations have called Mary blessed" (CCC 148).

Prayer

How are you blessed today? How can you approach the challenges of the day with a joyful mind-set? Embrace the Hail Mary as a lifeline to what matters most and pray it with that intention today.

Maria Morera Johnson is a CatholicMom.com *blogger, co-host of SPQN's* Catholic Weekend, *and author of* My Badass Book of Saints. *She blogs at MariaMJohnson.com.*

Blessed *art* thou among women

❦

Fr. James Tucker

God, through the archangel Gabriel, calls Mary first "full of grace" (or "highly favored one"). Then she is called "blessed" over and above all other women.

Art is a form of the verb *to be*. We recall from theological philosophy that God is being; God is existence itself. We, as created by God, share in his existence. So that while God *is* being itself, we *have* being. God, as transcendent, has power and authority over all he has created. If one has authority over what he has authored, then God has supreme authority over all creation. Thus, God can create the whole universe with the word that comes forth from his mouth; God can even fashion his own mother, thereby setting in motion our salvation. Finally, God can himself dwell among us as a human being, one of us. In his great wisdom, God has thus fashioned our salvation from sin and eternal death.

God set in motion our salvation through Jesus Christ, true God and true man, by using our human nature, indeed, our very human existence. For God did not simply strap on a human being costume the way we may put on a disguise. No, God adopted our human existence, right down to the molecular and genetic level, giving Jesus Christ a human heritage. This is why those long genealogies in the Gospels of Matthew and Luke are so important. They show Jesus as a true human being, with a heritage spanning and influencing history.

God, in his eternal authority, fashioned and chose Mary to be the catalyst for salvation in Jesus Christ. Mary was a created being through and through, just like us, except conceived without original sin.

What does this mean for us? The Old Testament tells us that God, as he led his people out of slavery in Egypt, tabernacled among them. He set up his tent, as it were, among his people. Yet he still showed himself as "the God of the high mountaintops," *El-Shaddai*. Just as high and inaccessible the high mountaintops were, even more so was God Almighty. No one could even touch the base of the mountain upon which God chose to reveal himself lest they be struck down.

God also chose to have his glorious presence descend upon the propitiatory, the cover of the Ark of the Covenant, that space between the two cherubim wings. The *Shekinah*, the cloud of glory, rendered the Ark of the Covenant itself inaccessible. The high priests had to carry it on poles but were never to touch it lest they die (2 Sm 6:6–7).

This incident could be the foundation for the Catholic conviction that Jesus had no other siblings by Mary. Mary is meant to be the fulfillment of the Old Testament Ark of the Covenant, carrying Jesus, who is the Bread of Life, the ultimate High Priest, and the Word of God. Just as no one was to touch the Ark upon which God's glory descended, so no one, not even Joseph, was to touch Mary, whom the Spirit of the Lord overshadowed (Lk 1:35).

Unlike the Ark of the Covenant, which was carried conspicuously in procession before the people of God, Mary lived her life in obscurity. Anyone sharing the streets of Nazareth with her would not have recognized Mary as the Mother of God. Yet she still retained that special lofty position that God had given her.

This relative obscurity benefits us in that Mary is more approachable as a human being, just as Jesus—true God and true man—is also accessible to us. To know that the Son of God had a mother puts our minds at ease. We all share this most important of human relationships. Most of us reserve a special place for the woman who gave us life—or, more accurately, shares that life-giving power with Almighty God. How much more blessed do we consider the one who gave life to the Son of God?

Prayer

God is among us. He isn't distant and neither is his Mother. In fact, God has been working on approachability for thousands of years. Are we responding to that? As you pray the Hail Mary today, picture Mary beside you, holding your hand and leading you closer to God, the person and beloved who longs for you.

Fr. James Tucker, a priest in the Archdiocese of Newark, New Jersey, is the founder of CatholicCreativity.net and manager of two other websites: FlashFiction.CatholicCreativity.net (showcasing short fiction of several authors) and CommentsfromtheKoala.com (a puppet video website for children).

Blessed art *thou* among women

Julie Davis

I reel off the Hail Mary like a pro these days. Twelve years ago, as a newly fledged convert, I was concentrating so hard on the overall prayer and meditation that I never gave smaller words like *thou* a second thought.

Thinking about it now, I realize that *thou* is anything but a small word. In fact, it may be one of the most important words in the Hail Mary.

Thou is the intimate, familiar form of the word *you* from Early Modern English. English used to be just like French and Spanish with both a formal and familiar form of the word *you*. I would have said *you* to my boss but called my husband *thou*. (Interesting side note: *thou* is the singular of *ye*, so I would have called my family *ye* as in "Ye all get in the car right now or we'll be late!")

We think of *thou* as biblical language because when William Tyndale translated the Bible into

English in the 1500s, he was trying to maintain the singular and plural distinctions found in the Hebrew and Greek originals. The King James Version followed suit, but everyday language was changing to use *you* exclusively for both singular and plural, familiar and formal settings. The Bible, therefore, became the last stronghold of *ye, thee, thy, thine,* and *thou.*

As interesting as that is, when I think of "Blessed art *thou* among women" it is as if I hear God tenderly speaking with great love through his messenger, the archangel Gabriel. *Thee, thou, thy* are everywhere in the prayer.

When I say those intimate, personal forms of *you,* am I speaking to Mary as my mother, my sister in Christ, my fellow disciple? The words are personal. How personal is my relationship?

The Hail Mary is my go-to prayer in times of anxiety, stress, and even when I'm just casting around for a prayer to say off the cuff. That's a bit odd, actually, because one of the things I struggle with is my lack of devotion to Mary. Oh, I appreciate her role, example, and life. In fact, I owe her a great debt of gratitude for pointing me toward a retreat that was a turning point for me. I just don't turn to her the way others do.

Looking at the tenderness of *thou* in this prayer, though, it occurs to me that it would behoove me to think more about all the words and let them draw me closer to Christ's Mother, and mine. That is something I will be meditating on every time the Hail Mary passes my lips.

Prayer

Is prayer just one more thing you cross off your to-do list? It's all too easy to turn our relationship with God, and the conversations that form that relationship, into a series of tasks to be accomplished. While that's better than nothing, pause today and pray the Hail Mary slowly. Let each word wash over you. Let yourself be struck by insight, interrupted by the prayer itself, and drawn into deeper relationship with God and his Mother as you pray the words.

Julie Davis was raised as an atheist but converted to Catholicism in 2000; she blogs at Happy Catholic *and podcasts at* A Good Story Is Hard to Find.

Blessed art thou *among* women

Jeffrey Miller

❧ ❧ ❧

Mary is blessed *among* women. Rather than indicating a separation of Mary from other women, it specifically casts her with other women. Mary is, as the poet Wordsworth referred to her, "Our tainted nature's solitary boast."

Mary is indeed among women. There are many types of Mary in the Old Testament; prominent among them is Eve. At least since the time of St. Justin Martyr, Mary has been seen as the new Eve. While the parallels with Eve are many, it is where the parallels break down that is most illustrative of the difference between them. As St. Irenaeus wrote, "The knot of Eve's disobedience was loosened by Mary's obedience. The bonds fastened by the virgin Eve through disbelief were untied by the virgin Mary through faith." Eve was the mother of all the living, and Mary is the mother of all the living in the order of grace. St. Jerome put the difference rather succinctly: "Death through Eve, life through Mary."

Other examples of types of Mary in the Old Testament include Sarah, Deborah, Miriam, Judith, and Esther. Esther especially was an intercessor who gave of herself in her role as queen. Mary, in her role of Queen Mother, fulfills that intercessory role expanded to include the Jewish people and all nations.

We don't have to look only in the Old Testament to find types of Mary. There are a plethora of women saints who in their devotion to the Blessed Virgin Mary came to resemble her in her obedience and love of Jesus.

It is one of the ironies of modern society that the Catholic Church is so often attacked as misogynic and accused of oppressing women while at the same time being criticized for talking so much about the Blessed Virgin. From the very beginning the Church has recognized the role of women. The Church boasts of the genius of St. Augustine and likewise boasts of the role of his mother, St. Monica.

Mary is the greatest among women and really is the "solitary boast" for both men and women. Mary is blessed among women, and the Church is also blessed with many great women. As Pope John Paul II wrote in his "Letter to Women":

> In this vast domain of service, the Church's two-thousand-year history, for all its historical conditioning, has truly experienced the

"genius of woman"; from the heart of the Church there have emerged women of the highest caliber who have left an impressive and beneficial mark in history. I think of the great line of woman martyrs, saints and famous mystics. In a particular way I think of Saint Catherine of Siena and of Saint Teresa of Avila, whom Pope Paul VI of happy memory granted the title of Doctors of the Church. And how can we overlook the many women, inspired by faith, who were responsible for initiatives of extraordinary social importance, especially in serving the poorest of the poor? The life of the Church in the Third Millennium will certainly not be lacking in new and surprising manifestations of "the feminine genius." (*Letter of Pope John Paul II to Women*, June 29, 1995)

Prayer

Whom are you among? Who most needs the effort of your Hail Mary today? Offer your prayer today for those in your life who may need it. Consider yourself in the company of Mary and the many women saints over the centuries.

Jeffrey Miller, a former atheist, shares his humorous and sometimes serious take on things religious and political on his award-winning blog SplendorofTruth.com/CurtJester.

Blessed art thou among

women

❧

Jennifer Fitz

I have never been a girly girl. Steeped from childhood in the androgynous, militant feminism of the 1970s, I came of age with a vague idea that femininity involved sexual license, athleticism, and a talent for mathematics. I aced calculus and played rugby, but I still argued bitterly with people who told me I was too smart to be just a housewife. Deep down I knew that being "just a mom" was more than enough for anybody.

When I returned to the Church in my twenties, married and longing for children, I lapped up old-school odes to traditional marriage roles and the complementarity of the sexes. Among Catholics there was the Marian twist, but still I found the explanations wanting: it seemed as if Christian femininity was all about lace tablecloths and lovely fingernails. I was real short in the fingernail department.

Four children later, puzzling over what this "woman thing" might be about, the answer is intuitive: motherhood. Not stay-at-home motherhood, not lovely-Thanksgiving-dinners motherhood, not fifteen-children-and-counting motherhood. Just motherhood. Just as Eve was called Eve before she ever conceived and gave birth, so Mary was prepared from her own conception to become mother of the Most High—a holy motherhood counted not from the moment she said yes to the archangel Gabriel, not from the day she gave birth in a stable, but from the very moment she existed.

Motherhood is who we are as women, regardless of whether we ever marry or ever conceive. Motherhood is the business of populating heaven. Men engender the little humans, and their part is not to be denigrated, but it is women who bear them. The first six or ten pounds of human flesh that come forth from the womb? That's Mom's flesh, born from Mom's body.

Men are, on average, larger and stronger than women. They are uniquely equipped to serve mothers and to protect, defend, and provide for the life that women bring forth. In fact, they come into their glory through this service. And so we rightly recognize the bravery and courage of men—a kind of bravery that is uniquely masculine, the fortitude of fatherhood.

But we deceive and cheat ourselves if we fall for the line that motherhood is weakness and fear. It is not. Not for a moment. To be a mother is to embrace risk. It is to hand over your very body, your very life, to the service of another in the hope—the mere hope—that the newly created soul will make its way to heaven, cooperating of its own free will with God's grace.

And if some of us women are called to biological motherhood—the business of bringing forth newly created bodies and souls—all of us are called to spiritual motherhood. Grandmother, aunt, sister, daughter, colleague—whatever our title, we have a lifelong mission. An eternal mission, as the intercession of the saintly women in heaven attests.

Which souls are you ushering toward heaven today? For whom are you praying? Whom are you serving? To whom are you showing the presence and the love of Christ? For whom do you offer up your last ounce of nothing, when all you have to offer is a pierced soul and a sorrowful heart? Motherhood is brave and risky business. Revel in the danger.

Prayer

We all have women in our lives who can use any amount of prayer that we can spend for them. Let's pray the Hail Mary today for women, and specifically for mothers of all stripes and types—those longing for motherhood and those living it in all its variations, those struggling through the daily hurdles, those who walk in sorrow and pain.

Jennifer Fitz, author of Classroom Management for Catechists, *writes about faith, family, and Christian discipleship at Patheos.com/blogs/JenniferFitz.*

and blessed is the fruit of thy womb, Jesus

Ginny Kubitz Moyer

When I was single, signing birthday cards was a straightforward process. At the end of my message, I'd scribble, "Love, Ginny," and that was that. Post-wedding, the process became a bit more complicated: "Love, Ginny," gave way to "Love, Ginny and Scott." With the exchange of vows, I'd acquired not just a new last name but a longer written sign-off.

Now, as the mother of two, signing a card is more complicated still: "Love, Ginny, Scott, Matthew, and Luke." It's no longer something I can dash off in three seconds; it takes more time, more space on the paper, and more muscle movement. Sometimes, when I'm feeling lazy, I just scrawl "Ginny, Scott, and boys." When *really* pressed for time, I'll make do with a quick "Ginny and Co."

But regardless of which option I choose, there's always an *and* in my sign-off. I'm no longer just one person but part of a unit. I'm part of a little family that, ten years ago, did not exist. And I like that.

Admittedly, there are times when it's not easy to be part of an *and*. On the rare days when we arrange a sitter and go to the movies, my husband wants to see the latest action flick while I would rather watch the movie about English women in bonnets and gloves. (Compromise ensues.) As a mom, I find that one of my kids invariably needs my attention just when I'm getting rolling on a writing project. Back when I was pregnant, the demands of being an *and* were even more taxing; there was a little person inside me who ate everything I ate and drank everything I drank (good-bye alcohol, normal amounts of caffeine, and Brie).

But when I really think about this word, I can't help but see it as a positive. *And* means more. It signifies abundance. It means that you are not alone but part of a family or a community. It means sharing a past, present, and future. It means having someone else there with you, by your side and on your side, through smooth sailing and through storms.

When I think about Mary, it's obvious that she knew all about being part of an *and*. In the Bible, we read about Mary and Joseph, Mary and Elizabeth, Mary and the beloved disciple, Mary and the apostles in the upper room. Throughout the gospels we catch numerous glimpses of a woman in relationship with others. Those relationships surely sustained her in moments of joy and wonder, in moments of confusion and uncertainty, in moments of excruciating pain—and in moments of astonishing new life.

Most of all, there's the relationship that we see depicted on Christmas cards and in art museums all over the world. It's the relationship between Madonna and child, Mary and Jesus, Mother and Son. It's about two people, one who grew inside the other, sharing a connection that is universal and intimate and beautiful. It's the *and* that has changed the world.

Prayer

We need others. And others need us. Some days, it's an overwhelming avalanche of need. Other times, it's an invisible thread binding us to them. Offer your Hail Mary today for all those whom you need and who need you, even those you may not know about.

Ginny Kubitz Moyer, author of Random MOMents of Grace *and* Mary and Me, *lives in the San Francisco Bay area and blogs at RandomActsofMomness.com.*

and *blessed* is the fruit of thy womb, Jesus

Michelle Reitemeyer

The graces obtained from the Sacrament of Marriage are vital," I said firmly to my Catholic acquaintance. "I doubt my marriage would have survived so long without them. And I see many troubled marriages . . . Catholic friends . . . not married in the Church. It's tough."

A long time passed, perhaps a year. One day, this same acquaintance reminded me of that conversation. "You got me thinking that day," she said. "I talked to my husband and we're going to be married in the Church next month." I had no idea that her marriage of over a decade had been performed by a justice of the peace. Had I known, I might never have said what I did, not wanting to offend her. I was humbled by her decision to obtain a sacramental marriage on account of my words. It wasn't my work. It was the Holy Spirit. You never know when he might use you.

I have also been on the receiving end of casual words that haunt me. The word *blessed* is one such word. I recall a brief encounter from more than a year ago. I was having a bad day made worse by the necessity of driving to my husband's office on a military post some twenty miles away. To get on post, you have to show your ID to a guard at a gate and most engage in some typical small talk.

The woman on duty asked me, "How are you today?" and I answered, "Fine, thank you," even though I didn't really mean it. I asked her, "How are you?" because I am polite, and because I really do care, in a small way, and strive hard to recognize that it is a person and not an automaton with whom I am dealing. And she answered, "I am blessed. Thank you for asking."

These are words I have pondered in my heart frequently in the last year or more. I could never recognize that woman again and I doubt she would remember me. I suspect that here, once again, the Holy Spirit was at work.

Could Elizabeth have known, two millennia ago, the power of her words? "Blessed are you," she told Mary, "and blessed is the fruit of your womb." We have scripture's confirmation that her words were the work of the Holy Spirit and that Mary dwelled on, if not these particular statements, certainly many other conversations and events surrounding the Incarnation.

I doubt Elizabeth expected her joyous exclamations to become the foundation of one of the most frequently recited prayers in history. I am confident, however, that Mary knew she was blessed. Unlike me, who on that grumpy day was not feeling particularly blessed and definitely needed a reminder, Mary was ever aware of God's infinite goodness. It is this awareness that we are all called to emulate.

It is not always easy to feel God's blessings. Many days, in fact, it is quite a challenge. But this is not a trivial glass-half-full change of attitude. There is nothing wrong with acknowledging the difficulties that life is handing us; we don't have to like our circumstances. But Mary's response to a "crisis pregnancy" and an awkward social situation was not wailing and gnashing of teeth. Rather, her spirit rejoiced in God her Savior, as Luke tells us.

This rejoicing in the midst of a difficult situation was a supreme act of humility. Mary could see that God was using her to fulfill his divine will and she was grateful for the honor. None of us are called to such service, yet we each have our own small role in God's plan. We can choose to be grumpy and ungrateful, or we can humbly accept God's blessings in whatever form they come.

Prayer

You are blessed. Do you know that? Do you appreciate it? Are you aware of the difference it makes in your life? Stop for a moment today and pray the Hail Mary, doing your best to be alert to how you are specifically blessed.

———————————————————

Michelle Reitemeyer is a military wife and homeschooling mother of seven.

and blessed *is* the fruit of thy womb, Jesus

Christine Johnson

What a daunting task, to contemplate the word *is*. How do you discuss the meaning of the verb *to be*? Have you tried defining it for a child? But here, in the middle of the Hail Mary, is this verb: *is*. *To be*. Conjugating the verb brings me up short, makes me stop in my tracks and realize something huge.

I am. This is God. "I am who I am" (Ex 3:14). The Great I AM. God, as Fr. Robert Barron puts it in his *Catholicism* series, has a nature of existence. His very nature is *to be*.

God has no beginning and no end. He is eternal. Alpha and Omega. These are things we hear and say, but to contemplate it is mind-numbing. I remember trying to understand this when I was a child. We were on a long trip from the Jersey Shore to Long Island to visit family, and I sat in the backseat of the car thinking about the eternal nature of God. I gave myself my very first headache. But to contemplate it here in the Hail Mary gives us new things to think about.

First, the eternal God, Creator of all things visible and invisible, became a human being. The Second Person of the Blessed Trinity, who has no beginning, had a beginning to his human life, and it was the moment the archangel Gabriel approached the Blessed Virgin Mary and heard her *fiat*.

But this portion of the Hail Mary comes not from Gabriel. This part is from St. Elizabeth, Mary's cousin, who has been confined to home as she awaits the birth of her first child, who will become the Baptizer. Elizabeth greets Mary with joy, proclaiming, "Blessed are you among women, and blessed is the fruit of your womb" (Lk 1:42).

And here is what sticks out to me: Elizabeth's verb tense. Blessed *is* the fruit of your womb. Elizabeth doesn't say, "Blessed will be the fruit of your womb." She doesn't use past tense, either, saying, "Blessed has been the fruit of your womb." She uses the present tense: blessed *is*.

Jesus, new in Mary's womb and yet Ancient of Days, *is* blessed. Blessed be the name of God! Blessed be his holy name! We should be in continual praise of God, blessing his name at all times. Every breath we have—every thought, word, and deed of our lives—should be given over to praise of our Creator! Elizabeth does just this. She blesses God, giving him praise and thanksgiving.

The second thing that is brought to my mind as I look at this verb is that Jesus is present at that moment. Again, he is newly formed. When Mary receives word of Elizabeth being pregnant, Elizabeth is already in her sixth month. Mary would be traveling around 115 miles to get there. That's a day trip for us, but riding on an ass there and back, it's hardly an easy journey. But even if it took a month, Mary would be only about six weeks pregnant by the time she arrived at Elizabeth's home in present-day Ein Karem. This is a time when no one would be able to tell that Mary was pregnant just by looking at her. Jesus would be so tiny—less than an inch in length—that some people today would even question whether he was really a baby yet. Elizabeth uses the present tense verb to refer to Mary's hidden Child. Jesus is present there—Emmanuel, God with us.

And this brings us to a final point: very often, we cannot see God with us. We look and find nothing. Our sorrows overwhelm us, and we fear drowning in our fears and anxieties. But Jesus is with us. He might be hidden from obvious sight, as he was when Mary went to visit her cousin, but he is near.

He is with you in a friend who calls just when you need someone to talk to. He is with you in the article you come across that speaks perfectly to your situation. He is with you in that tweet that makes you laugh in spite of your sadness. He is even with you in the smile of a stranger you pass in the store. We need only to seek him, and he will reveal himself to us, often in very surprising ways.

Is. It's such a small word, but like the whispering wind that Elijah heard at the mouth of the cave (1 Kgs 19:11–13), it's not to be overlooked. After all, it is who God says he is.

Prayer

What is your sorrow, your sadness, your grief? What burden do you carry within you? Can you, like Elizabeth at the Visitation, see that God is with you? Pray the Hail Mary today and bare yourself to Mary. Let her lead you to the comfort of her Son.

Christine Johnson is a Lay Dominican who blogs at Domestic Vocation *and is a regular contributor to* CatholicMom.com. *She lives in the beautiful Blue Ridge Mountains of Virginia.*

and blessed is **the** fruit of thy womb, Jesus

Jaymie Stuart Wolfe

The: a word far more often said than prayed.

There are many languages that do not have the word *the* at all. Latin, Sanskrit, Hindi, Japanese, Russian: all these do without it. But for English speakers, saying or not saying *the* matters. For us, there is an expansive difference between what we mean when we say "one" and "*the* one." *The* is how we distinguish what is set apart and above. It is how we express singularity, uniqueness, excellence. *The* tells us that all the things we may consider alike are not quite as alike as we had thought. *The* communicates that there is something that sums up everything—a one-of-a-kind reality that defines and fully expresses the essence of that reality.

In this case, it is "*the* fruit of thy womb." There is only one fruit like this one, and that is why there is only one womb like Mary's. This phrase in the Hail Mary originates in the mouth of Elizabeth (Lk 1:42).

Like Mary's, Elizabeth's pregnancy is miraculous. "This is the sixth month for her who was called barren" (Lk 1:36). But still, there is a difference. There is no pregnancy like Mary's because there is no child like hers. The fruit of Mary's womb is *the* fruit.

The: too small to notice and easily forgotten.

A young girl in an obscure town at the edge of an empire. A virgin. A Jew. Poor. Overlooked and overlookable. To say that no one would have given her a second glance would presume that someone would have taken notice of her at all. "And the virgin's name was Mary" (Lk 1:27).

The: useful, but with no significance in itself.

But Someone did notice. God had set his heart on her. To him, Mary was not too small to be remembered, nor too low to be exalted. To God, Mary was not someone to be used as a kind of divine surrogate. He did not see her as someone who could play a scripted part in the drama of salvation and then walk off the stage when her lines were finished. God chose to love Mary in a remarkable way, to include her in his life as mother. "For he has looked upon his handmaid's lowliness" (Lk 1:48).

The: never standing alone.

Mary never stands alone. When we see her, she is with the angel, with Elizabeth, with Joseph, with Jesus. She is found where people gather, not lagging behind them or leading them, but already there.

Mary is seen at the crib and at the cross. She is waiting in the Upper Room and in heaven.

The: tucked into the middle of the prayer as it ascends to its centerpiece and single most important word, Jesus.

Mary lives on the threshold of salvation. She is the gate, the door, the hinge for God's saving grace as it enters the world. Her life unfolds near the center of human history. That center has a name: Jesus. Mary does not merely point us to Jesus or lead us to him. Mary brings him to us, wrapped in swaddling clothes, wrapped in a shroud, wrapped in the shining cloud of God's glory. Mary bears Jesus: to meet her is to encounter her Son, *the* only begotten Son of God, "*the* way and *the* truth and *the* life" (Jn 14:6).

Prayer

It's hard to be humble, especially when we are surrounded with all the busyness and bustle, the demands of more, more, more. All of that tempts us to focus on ourselves exclusively, to prioritize ourselves and our desires, to see ourselves as more important than Jesus. Think of one small act of humility you can offer up for Jesus today and, if you can, do it while you pray your Hail Mary.

Jaymie Stuart Wolfe, a wife, mother of eight, and Catholic convert, echoes God's universal call to holiness through her work as an author, columnist, speaker, musician, and full-time editor at Pauline Books & Media.

and blessed is the *fruit* of thy womb, Jesus

Pat Gohn

Bite into any lush, ripened, fresh fruit and you feel the gush of juice between your lips and running down along your tongue to the little well underneath. You move the pulpy flesh of the fruit around in your mouth, gliding it in place with your tongue to chew it. Depending on the variety of fruit, you may experience momentary dripping down your cheek or lower dimples as you savor the flavor and enjoy that first full bite.

The fruit was where the trouble started. One taste of the fruit of the tree—the tree that God had expressly forbidden (Gn 3:2–3)—and Eve was in deep trouble.

One bite of the fruit and Eve was mesmerized. Her knowledge grew immediately, but in ways she did not expect. She expected to be like God; duped, instead she became a lesser mortal than before. The preternatural gifts she was endowed with by her Creator were shut down. No longer blessed with infused knowledge, she could not see the truth of her present situation. She gave the fruit to Adam.

The woman, the fruit gatherer and eventual fruit bearer, unwittingly tasted decay and death disguised as a temporary tasty morsel that slid down the back of her throat. The mother of all the living had triggered the trapdoor leading to separation from God and eventual suffering and death. Her husband, unable to withstand the temptation, also acquiesced and took a bite.

We know the rest of the story.

The divine will and providence of God so loved the man and the woman and their progeny—us!—that he sent them a way out of their plight. But first God would cultivate a new fruit, and a new fruit bearer. The Woman, the one that God envisioned from the start (Gn 3:15), would one day bear the fruit that saves humanity from its sins.

It was St. Irenaeus who taught that the knot Eve tied was untied by Mary. St Louis de Montfort also spoke a deep truth: "The salvation of the whole world began with the 'Hail Mary.' Hence, the salvation of each person is also attached to this prayer."

Only Mary, God's pure and perfect creature, the masterpiece of creation, could bear such good fruit, both in word and deed. Jesus, the offspring of the Virgin's womb, was indeed the blessed fruit of a remarkable holy union—the sign and promise of the wedding of God to his creation.

We sing of it with every note of "Ave Maria" and pray it with every syllable of the Hail Mary! The fruit we sing of and adore in the center of this prayer is the vital and everlasting fruit of Mary's womb, *Jesus*! The fruit—Jesus—would sweeten and strengthen humanity, answering every angelic prayer of heaven and long-suffering mortal supplication of earth since that fateful day in the garden.

Not surprisingly, we can understand why the fruit that is Jesus would one day be eaten. Jesus would lay his own flesh down to be food, and those who eat of it would partake of eternity (Jn 6:35–58; Lk 22:19). Down through the ages the flesh of that miraculous fruit would feed apostles and martyrs, kings and saints, rich and poor, poets and psalmists, young and old, saints and sinners, you and me.

No longer would a fruit bring a curse. No longer would the thirst of sin go unquenched.

Blessed is the fruit that revives the soul and restores true life—the good fruit, the holy fruit, the succulent fleshy fruit of God's own nature mingling with our own, its juice running down our chin, nourishing our bodies, transforming our lot with its precious wine.

Prayer

How are you fruitful? What do you offer God? Are you willing to give it freely and completely, to let it be used up or consumed, to allow him to pass it on to someone else? Pray the Hail Mary with an open heart today, asking God to make you fruitful for his purpose.

Pat Gohn is a wife and a mother to three grown children. She holds a master's degree in theology and shares her faith as a columnist, speaker, host of the Among Women *podcast, and author of* Blessed, Beautiful, and Bodacious.

and blessed is the fruit of thy womb, Jesus

Lisa M. Hendey

My ponderings of the word *of* remind me of some of the best words I've ever heard on praying the Rosary. If the following excerpt sounds familiar to you, it's perhaps because I shared this same bit of wisdom in *The Handbook for Catholic Moms* in my chapter on Mary. The author is my favorite Irish pastor, Msgr. Michael Collins, who I sincerely hope now has at least one little toe out of purgatory and into heaven. The following should be read with the lilting Irish accent of a ninety-two-year-old parish priest who was about to meet his Maker: "Please say the Rosary. I've always been afraid of hell, I don't like hell, but I'm convinced that if I'm true to the Rosary, which I have been—I've said the Rosary ever since I was a child, I've never deliberately missed the Rosary and I don't say that as a boast, I say that as kind of an assurance—that if I ask the Blessed Mother fifty times a day to be with me now and at the hour of my death, she'll be around somewhere to take me home."

Simple thoughts, a simple prayer made up of a handful of short, simple words. Yet when collected together, they hold the ticket to such profound grace. Yes, our Blessed Mother is there for us to lead us to the fruit *of* her womb, Jesus Christ.

What a blessing to know with such confidence, as Msgr. Collins did, that she who loved—and continues to love—with such tenderness through so much pain has unending patience with my shortcomings. Forty-two words, recited in a matter of minutes, and yet how often I rattle through them mindlessly, neglecting the grace of each syllable—even of that second *of*—or forgetting them altogether in my busyness.

They deserve such awe, such reverence, and such thanksgiving. Each of them, collected together in our hearts and expressed in confident love, takes us home.

Prayer

There are so many ways we fail each day. In each attempt we make for God, we fall short. How can we possibly accomplish what he wants for us when we are limited by our nature and our being? That's the beauty of it, though. Every small part, every tiny piece, has a part to play. Pray the Hail Mary today and let it be a doorway to the smallest successes you can offer to God.

Lisa M. Hendey speaks internationally on faith, family, and technology and is the founder of CatholicMom.com *and author of* The Grace of Yes.

and blessed is the fruit of *thy* womb, Jesus

Dorian Speed

What's so special about Mary?

That's the question that the word *thy* provokes in me—a memory of myself as the pettiest of teacher's pets, grousing in my room about why Mary gets all the attention. What about *me*? I am in the green group for reading, and I can play *three* hymns on the piano, and I *always* get chosen to write names on the board when the teacher is out of the room. Why should *Mary* get all this attention?

I'm happy to report this memory dates back to 1981, but I must admit I still struggle with the same sins—pride, jealousy, selfishness. And though I've matured a bit since first grade, I do still find Mary a bit of a mystery. My affection for her has grown, particularly since becoming a mother myself. At the same time, I understand why some find Marian devotion baffling at best.

So what is so special about Mary? It comes down to two words—*fiat* and *magnificat*.

Fiat—"let it be done." She lived her life in perfect unity with the will of God. This is so difficult for me to wrap my mind around, particularly since becoming a mother myself—to imagine myself at the foot of the cross, not lashing out at the crowd but offering up a heart pierced by a sword. I can't understand her forgiveness, and I can't understand her humility, but I can look to her as a model of both.

Magnificat—from *Magnificat anima mea Dominum*—"my soul declares the greatness of the Lord." She held nothing back—no hidden corner of her soul where she kept her list of grudges, no gloating over her perfection. And because she devoted her entire being to God, her life was a reflection of his glory.

Every once in a blue moon, I understand what this means—my soul rejoices in the glory of God. Triggers include sweet baby kisses, tomatoes that actually taste like tomatoes, and a gap-toothed grin on a face full of freckles. And I see that my soul is proclaiming the glory of the Lord not because I did something super amazing but because I am allowing myself to cooperate fully with him at that moment.

This, then, is what makes Mary unique, and if I can take my mind off myself long enough to contemplate her fullness of grace, perhaps I can bring a little more *fiat* and *magnificat* into my own life.

Prayer

It's so much easier to make big plans and set huge goals than it is to focus on the small steps we need to take to get up the mountain before us. Saying yes to the big question might be far easier than the yes for the small inconveniences or the tiny disruptions of the day. Offer your Hail Mary for the yes God is asking from you today, even if it's a tiny three-letter whisper and not a loud shout.

Dorian Speed writes from the suburbs of Houston, where she homeschools her three children while working as a web developer and volunteering for too many things. Her writing can be found at Scrutinies.net, CatholicMom.com, Dappled Things literary magazine, and various other places.

and blessed is the fruit of thy *womb*, Jesus

Kevin Lowry

Womb. What a great word. Of course, we don't actually use the word much anymore. It's a *uterus* or, worse, an *oven* (as in, "she's got a bun in the oven").

The word *womb* itself has esoteric connotations. For a man, writing about the womb is like trying to write about the joys of shopping, or why crying can be a good thing, or why women go to the bathroom at the same time when they're together at a restaurant. We men don't get it at all.

Yet here's what impresses me about the womb in the context of the Hail Mary. In a very practical, concrete sense (that even a guy can grasp), Mary's assent to the angel at the Annunciation gave God a big thumbs-up to change her from within. Of course, this would be manifested externally soon enough, and Mary was certainly aware of the possible ramifications. But she said yes anyway.

In my conversion to the Church, the thing that first caught my attention was the teaching on artificial birth control. At the time, I was Presbyterian, and the topic was a nonissue. After questioning (at some length) what substances my classmates at Franciscan University were inhaling or otherwise ingesting, I had to listen. At least well enough to pass the class. Sex has something to do with babies? Actions have consequences? Responsibility? It was all quite appalling.

Later, some guy named Scott Hahn gave me a rosary. I had no idea what it was. But there I was, and I had the audacity and lack of judgment to use it. What was I thinking? You know where this all leads—my wife and I faced the inevitable and entered the Church. We have eight kids.

Wouldn't you know it, twenty years later, I still don't fully understand the Hail Mary—but it's my favorite prayer. And I know one thing—without the women in my life who opened their wombs out of love, I wouldn't be who I am today. Or I wouldn't *be* at all.

I'm a rather obtuse guy, for sure, but also one who wants more than anything to give God a thumbs-up to change me from within—not via a womb, of course, but in my interior, spiritual life. To be more like the next word in the Hail Mary—the Word Incarnate himself. Jesus.

Prayer

Change can only begin from within. Sometimes we change and no one even notices because the change is so interior that they can't possibly see it. The large oak started as a tiny acorn. Let the change God's asking from you begin with today's Hail Mary.

Kevin Lowry is a business executive, speaker, and the author of Faith at Work: Finding Purpose beyond the Paycheck. *Find out more at GratefulConvert.com.*

and blessed is the fruit of thy womb, *Jesus*

Walt Staples

In reciting the Hail Mary, at the end of the second sentence, one comes to the word that is the point of the whole exercise, *Jesus*. This fruit of Mary's womb smiles back at me from the arms of the Bavarian Virgin on my desk as she dances with her child, just as I watched my wife dance with our children when they were babes.

But who is this Jesus?

Is he the Victorian Jesus who appears to say, "There, there," and seems to be trying to reassure the comfortable? Is he the angry rebel Jesus of the Jackson Browne song who appears to snarl at these same comfortable people? Is he the confused, swept away Jesus of Andrew Lloyd Webber and Tim Rice's depiction on Broadway?

Is he the deeply moved Jesus, with his arms thrown around one of the faithful who made it to that reward above all others, in the painting that draws sneers from the supercool? Is he the tired, smelly, wood-shaving-covered workman at the end of a long day as suggested by one thoughtful priest? Is he the friendly, fun-to-be-around guest at the marriage feast as shown by the pen-and-ink drawing known as the *Laughing Christ*?

Is he the wise rabbi who is sharp with those who know better but gentle with those who don't? Is he the agonized, bleeding man suffering because of the sins each of us commit with little thought, that is represented by a Spanish bust? Is he the baby smiling at me as his mother gaily dances barefoot with him on my desk?

Perhaps he is all of these. Man is a finite creature attempting to get his or her head around the Infinite. We are able to catch only facets of this visible part of the Trinity at the best of times, not because he keeps himself hidden from us, but rather because of our own limitations.

H. G. Wells used the metaphor of a fox attempting to understand a steam locomotive in his book *The War of the Worlds*. We often seem to be in the same position when we try to understand the Infinite. But, unlike Wells's fox, we have something going for us; we are God's children—he tells us so quite often. And, like children, we have the capacity to learn as we mature. This holds out the hope that when we each finally meet up with Jesus—some by direct route, most via purgatory—we'll understand a lot more.

Prayer

What's the point? Do you ever wonder that to yourself, feeling despair or hopelessness or just plain frustration? Pray today's Hail Mary and let go of all of that. Let it waft to heaven on the backs of the words of the prayer. Let God carry the burden and free yourself to recognize the reason for it all: Jesus himself.

A former president of the Catholic Writers Guild, Walt Staples published short stories on Avenir Electia, Rocket Science for the Rest of Us, and other websites until his death in 2012.

~~Holy~~ Mary, Mother of God

Karina Fabian

I have a lot of friends, especially through Facebook and other groups, who don't hesitate to ask for prayers for themselves or those they know. And I have just as many who are glad to say prayers for me or my family and friends in times of need. Prayer does more than send a message to God; it gives us comfort, even if it's just the comfort of knowing someone is laying our aching hearts in God's tender hands.

Yet there is something special about asking Mary to pray for us, and it comes down to the word *holy*. Mary was a woman like any woman, and at the same time, she was something more. God chose her, and in her beautiful, holy sacrifice of bearing his Son, she chose him in a way no other woman can. She shares an ineffable closeness with the Trinity: handmaid of the Father, vessel of the Spirit, mother of the Son. Her being and her actions brought her to holiness.

When Mary prays for us, she is more than offering comfort or sending a message to our Lord. She is also holding our hearts in her hands, the same hands that caressed Jesus' brow and comforted him as a baby. She is pressing them upon him as a parent might give a child something precious and alive to hold. She loves with a heart big enough to embrace the world because becoming the Mother of God gave her that ability.

Mary is not God or a goddess, as some people claim we Catholics think. But she is something more than a woman, more than a saint.

She is holy.

Prayer

Being called holy isn't necessarily a compliment, is it? And yet that's what we're called to be. That's the example Mary gives us. Pray the Hail Mary today for an increase in holiness that you may strive to be closer to Jesus through his mother.

Karina Fabian is a cradle Catholic and lifelong geek who has written devotionals, saint stories, science fiction about nuns in outer space, and a fantasy series about a Catholic dragon detective.

Holy *Mary*, Mother of God

Barb Szyszkiewicz

How many of the contributors to this wonderful collection have mentioned a woman's influence in their own devotion, usually a mother or grandmother? I haven't counted, but it seems like there have been quite a few. Here's one more.

Growing up, I spent a lot of time at my grandmother's house. I loved to visit her and even remember telling her that when I grew up I was going to move in! There was no doubt that her home was a Catholic home. "My" chair in the kitchen faced a picture of Our Lady of Perpetual Help, an image that to this day makes me think of my grandmother. After she died, I put a holy card with this image on my kitchen windowsill so that my kitchen, too, would be graced by the Blessed Mother.

My grandmother's kitchen was the heart of her home, and not just because she made the world's best potato salad and roast chicken there. More importantly, she did her praying there.

Through her example, she showed me the importance of being dedicated to daily prayer. She had an envelope full of holy cards with prayers and novenas on the back and would work through the entire stack daily. It was part of her routine; it was integral to her life. When one of us kids would come into the kitchen bursting with a story or a riddle to tell, she'd listen a moment and then quietly remind us, "I'm saying my prayers," and we'd wander off and try to silently raid the candy dish until she finished. She didn't yell at us to stop interrupting, no matter how many times we did.

Those quiet witnesses in the kitchen really stuck with me. My grandmother wove prayer into her daily life. What an example to set for her family!

It is in my own kitchen, not surprisingly, that I feel closest to Mary. It is there that I serve my family, just as Mary once served hers. It's a place of work and a place of prayer.

Prayer

Where do you feel closest to Mary? Perhaps it's a room in your house, a specific church or chapel, or a special spot outdoors. Go to that place today and pray the Hail Mary. Let Mary sit with you and guide you closer to her Son.

Barb Szyszkiewicz is a wife, mother, and Secular Franciscan who spends her days writing, cooking, reading, and substitute teaching. Find out more at FranciscanMom.com.

Holy Mary, of God

Michelle Buckman

*M*other. A multitude of emotions are attached to that word, universal and yet uniquely built on each individual's life experiences.

Mother conjures up flashes of childhood memories: bedtime stories and birthday parties, learning to swim, learning to ride a bike, and letting go of mother's hand to spend the night at a friend's house for the first time. High school and learning to drive, wanting freedom and then wanting to be held after a ruined friendship, hurt feelings, a day that seems like the end of the world.

Mother is there for all of it, good and bad, ups and downs, bound by heartstrings that we often take for granted until we are called to that same path and gaze upon our own child. Then we understand it all in a whole new way: an immeasurable love that guides us as we learn by trial and error how to fill the same role in a new way, a new world, a new reality. So much joy! First smiles, first words, first steps. So much anxiety! First fever, first fall, first fight.

My favorite scene in *The Passion of the Christ* is the flashback Mary has of Jesus scraping his knee as a child. Mary rushes to Jesus' side to comfort him. I like to think of Mary that way, the humanness of their relationship, the everyday mothering that still continues today: boo-boos and washing and preparing meals.

Mary taught Jesus to walk. She listened to his jokes and told him stories. And she lost track of him for a bit when all the cousins got together. (Take a parent's normal panic over losing track of a child and add on the image of God showing up and asking where his Son is!)

I like to think about her cuddling him in her lap and telling him stories, of making him wash behind his ears, and sewing his clothes. But I also like to think about later years, that sweet time when a boy develops into a man but still needs his mama and wants to take a walk with her down a country road or have a chat in the shade of an old oak tree.

Mary watched Jesus grow up and nudged him onto his path at the wedding in Cana. Then she stood aside, likely knowing where his path would lead. Did Jesus tell her what was going to happen? Did they lie on a hillside under the stars at night and confide in each other?

As Catholics, we have been raised to understand Mary in that endearing way. We embrace her not only because of the important role she played but also because we know she can sympathize with our family problems.

Christians often ask, "What would Jesus do?" But I also like to ponder, "What would Mary do?" because she understands the demands of motherhood. Mary has walked this path and knows there is nothing more challenging or more rewarding for a woman than being a mother.

Prayer

Look at the biggest problem you face today. Pray the Hail Mary and ask Mary for her guidance as you consider it.

Michelle Buckman, a writer and freelance editor, is the author of six novels, including the CALA winner Rachel's Contrition *and Christy Award finalist* Maggie Come Lately. *Find out more at www.MichelleBuckman.com.*

Holy Mary, Mother of God

Val J. Bianco

Of is a preposition, meaning "from." It can indicate ownership or position, neither of which has any meaning unless the word forms a bridge between two other words. Here, those words are *Mother* and *God*.

I have long felt that there is no human relationship that so closely mirrors the love of God for man as that of a mother for her child. Sadly, the inversion of this most perfect of human loves, abortion, would seem to be the magnum opus of Satan. In the Mother of God, however, this relationship is elevated to the pinnacle of human love. No two human beings ever have, or will, approach this level of being of each other. And so this *of* forms the bridge between the perfection of humanity and perfection itself.

Mary is *of* God in that she is *from* him, and in her *fiat* she completely belongs *to* him. Jesus, in turn, is *of* her in that his humanity springs forth *from* her. His genetic code, eyes, hair color, blood type, and smile are all *of* his mother, Mary. She nursed him, changed him, made his favorite foods, prayed with him, and sang him to sleep. Our Lady heard his first breath and his last. He was hers, and hers alone, until she gave him to humanity, even as he gave her hers.

Mary's divine Son, Jesus, was truly *of* her in a way that I will never understand, for only another mother can fully do so.

Can there be any clearer indication of this binding link than Cana? Mother *of* God, God *of* Mother. The first empirical evidence that this carpenter's son was God seemed little more than a magic trick. No one was healed; no one was saved. Seems kind of insignificant for the Messiah's first miracle. Why? The answer is Mary. She says, "They have no wine." He responds, "Woman, how does your concern affect me? My hour has not yet come." And she instructs the stewards as she has throughout history, speaking her heart's only desire: "Do whatever he tells you" (Jn 2:3–5).

Can it be coincidence that John records this dialogue? I think not. I believe that Cana, in its primacy, is a gift to us, a lesson in *of*. It is a clear reminder of the awesome power of a mother: the power to literally change God's mind! This, to me, is the full weight of the twenty-eighth word of the Hail Mary. Humble *of*, the bridge between the words *Mother* and *God*, the bridge between divinity and humanity, without which heaven would have been utterly unattainable.

Prayer

A few letters can make the meaning of a sentence completely different. In the same way, small efforts, little actions, and tiny contributions can build bonds that become unbreakable. Our lives can feel unimportant, but as we pray the Hail Mary today, let's ask for the grace to be an instrument of God just as Mary was, in whatever big—or small—way that God has in mind.

Val J. Bianco is a husband, father of ten, grandfather of fourteen, and author of the contemporary Catholic novel Sons of Cain.

Holy Mary, Mother of *God*

꩜

Arwen Mosher

The funny thing about the word *God* in the Hail Mary prayer is that Mary herself would not have been allowed to say it.

Well, more than not being allowed, she would not have wanted to. The Blessed Mother was a reverent woman, and it is forbidden for Jews to speak the name of God, the tetragrammaton (transliterated YHWH) that refers to God in Hebrew. I find it ironic, and highly symbolic, that every time we ask for her intercession in the Hail Mary we speak our form of a word that she would have avoided out of love and respect for God.

It's ironic because we say the Hail Mary out of love and respect for God. He wants us to ask for his grace through the prayers of his mother. In that act, we do something that she never would have done—with exactly the same motivation.

And it's symbolic because the Hail Mary prayer itself, just like Mary's whole life, from her immaculate conception through her *fiat* and her great sorrow to her eventual assumption into heaven, points to God. She lived for him, and because she did, her Son was able to die to save us. No solely human person has ever served God better.

Because she said yes and helped God bring Jesus into the world, we can now say the name of God aloud every time we pray. In our creed, we name the entire Trinity—Father, Son, Holy Spirit—with love and reverence. The new covenant, brought about in part because of Mary's love and obedience, makes us free to name the One who holds us in being.

God belongs in the Hail Mary because Mary's life is about God. Praise him for creating her so that we can have a chance to do as the servants of God before Christ could not: say his name.

Prayer

There isn't a lot of respect for the word *God* anymore. Today, as you pray the Hail Mary, consider how you might show God respect.

Arwen Mosher is a Michigan native and a happily married mother of four young children who loves to write almost as much as she loves answering her kids' questions about God.

pray for us sinners

Miriel Thomas Reneau

Perhaps more than any other prayer, the Hail Mary is the means by which we invoke the Blessed Mother's intercession. A single Rosary elicits those three powerful words dozens and dozens of times: "Pray for us . . . pray for us . . . pray for us." In that light, it might seem natural for the reflection on prayer in the Hail Mary to highlight Mary's role as our intercessor, as the saint who prays most fervently and most effectively on our behalf for the graces we need to live the Christian life.

But there is another connection between the Blessed Mother and prayer, a connection that jumped out at me more vividly than ever before as I was preparing to write this piece. In his apostolic letter *Rosarium Virginis Mariae*, Pope John Paul II calls the Rosary "the school of Mary." At this school, he goes on to say, we are "led to contemplate the beauty on the face of Christ and to experience the depths of his love." *Ad Jesum per Mariam* (to Jesus through Mary): always, always, Mary leads us to union with Christ.

Thus, as we ask her to intercede for us, Mary serves as a model for our own prayer, for the ways in which we relate to God. So when we think about the word *pray* in the context of the Hail Mary, the question arises: How does Mary pray? There are probably more answers than I can count—and certainly more than we have room for here—but meditating on a few of my favorite mysteries of the Rosary led me to some preliminary thoughts.

The Annunciation

I've always loved the account of the Annunciation in St. Luke's gospel (Lk 1:26–38), partly because it helps me to remember how human Mary is. Confronted with a strange situation, Mary is troubled; when the angel declares that she will bear a Son named Jesus, her first response is to ask him how this could be. And yet, despite her confusion and the dangers she has to know will accompany the mysterious events that Gabriel describes to her, Mary responds with faith. She conquers the natural impulse to fear with her confidence in her loving Father. And her *fiat* is not simply a grant of permission; it is also a prayer, a heartfelt petition that this mysterious divine plan will be realized in her life.

Meditating on Mary's actions at the moment of the annunciation helps me remember two things about prayer. First, obedience does not require us to be automatons; Mary's example shows that natural emotional responses to difficult situations do not automatically preclude the mastery of fear and anxiety by virtue and the genuine, ongoing surrender of our wills to the will of the Father. This is very good news for people like me. Second, she reminds me that one of the surest ways to accomplish this surrender is to pray for it to happen. We can say, "Let it be done unto me" before we possess the grace to really want it to be done. God will fill in the gaps.

The Nativity

The account of Christ's birth in the book of Luke tells us only two things about Mary's actions in that moment. We read first, "She gave birth to her firstborn son. She wrapped him in swaddling clothes and laid him in a manger" (2:7). These are such sparse words—too few, arguably, to do justice to such a glorious event. But then, after the shepherds' visit, we get another glimpse at the Blessed Mother. The text says, "All who heard it were amazed by what had been told them by the shepherds. And Mary kept all these things, reflecting on them in her heart" (2:18–19).

It seems to me that the quiet, simple description of Mary's reactions to the birth of Jesus shows us something about the value of quiet, simple prayer. In the face of the majesty of God, it might seem natural to respond with an overflow of fancy words. If a blogger had written the gospel account of the Nativity, it probably would have included a lot more adjectives. But maybe sometimes the appropriate response to incomprehensible divine mystery is not to try to describe it. Maybe the appropriate response is to hush.

The Wedding at Cana

I think of the wedding at Cana whenever I'm tempted to panic. Usually these temptations have to do with relatively minor situations—an interview or a paper deadline—but occasionally I'm faced with bigger worries. No matter what the details are, though, it always consoles me to think of that day in a small town in Galilee, when the absence of a good thing threatened to mar a joyful celebration. It is easy to think of this as a cosmically insignificant problem: nobody was going to die for lack of another glass of wine. But then I remember: our Lord came not simply that we may have life but that we may have it abundantly (Jn 10:10). At Cana, this is where the Blessed Mother comes in. She observes a need and, eschewing anxiety, gently points it out to her Son. Not, "Oh no, the wine is gone, whatever shall we do?" But, simply, "They have no wine." And then, to the servants, "Do whatever he tells you" (Jn 2:3–5).

I love this story because it shows me something about the nature of God. The Blessed Mother knows the Lord more intimately than any other human being, so we can trust that she knows how to approach him. And notice her behavior when she discovers a need: she is fearless. By her example, Mary teaches us to approach the throne of God confidently, trusting completely in his love and mercy. It is a reminder that I think many of us need more than we realize: God wants good things for us! And from this position of childlike confidence, we can understand her direction to do whatever he tells us. If God is trustworthy, if we believe that he wants good for us even more than we want it for ourselves, then we can persevere through any difficulty and obey any commandment. Mary's actions at Cana confirm and encourage us in that belief.

Pray and Learn

In the section of *Rosarium Virginis Mariae* titled "Learning Christ from Mary," Pope John Paul II makes the following observation about the Rosary: "This school of Mary is all the more effective if we consider that she teaches by obtaining for us in abundance the gifts of the Holy Spirit, even as she offers us the incomparable example of her own 'pilgrimage of faith.'" This is the beauty of Marian prayer: that the pedagogy of the Blessed Mother intertwines with her intercession. May we benefit from both as we seek to grow in the knowledge and love of her Son.

Prayer

Each day, we've been sitting with Mary and speaking to God. Our prayer has been woven together, woven into a tapestry that will lead us closer to our Creator. As we pray the Hail Mary today, let's sit a moment longer in his presence. Let's let ourselves be open to what he has to give us in this instant.

Miriel Thomas Reneau, a wife, new mother, and PhD candidate in American politics, lives, works, plays, and prays in Minnesota with her husband, John, and adorable baby, Gregory.

pray us sinners

Lisa Mladinich

If we want peace of heart, we must learn to forget ourselves and serve. So many people in our world are in constant pain because they live their lives in a state of perpetual uncertainty. Where did I come from? Where am I going? What is my life for?

They waste time rebelliously seeking status instead of meaning, pleasure instead of joy. They proudly resist the holy submission that would bring them lasting peace, while precious years roll by in an agony of emptiness as they drag others down with them—the very ones they were made to love and serve.

Like a good mother, our Blessed Mother bends to teach us that we are made *for* God, to love and serve him in this life and to spend all of eternity with him in the joy of heaven. Mary is a perfect model of loving service. Everything she does is *for* someone else. Because her soul is filled with grace, there is no room *for* sin to take root. Her self has been abandoned in a paradoxical love story in which she has let go of everything except her love *for* God and her trust in his love *for* her. God responds by filling her to overflowing with his glory.

Mother Teresa, perhaps one of the greatest saints of all time, was known to frequently pray, "Mary, give me your heart: so beautiful, so pure, so immaculate; your heart so full of love and humility that I may be able to receive Jesus in the Bread of Life and love him as you love him and serve him in the distressing guise of the poor."

Mary does all *for* her Son. She does all *for* us. She is *for* us, watching over us, teaching us to live our lives more abundantly in Jesus Christ. We can ask her anything, even to do those things we should do ourselves. We even ask her to pray *for* us!

To pray *for* someone is to give yourself in prayer on their behalf, but it is also to pray in their stead, to donate your own prayerfulness in their place. Our Lady is so worthy that her prayers *for* us outweigh all our limitations, engulfing our needs in her grace-filled pleas.

So what are we waiting for? Let us pray! Here's a prayer from St. Bernard of Clairvaux that we can use:

> Mother Mary, we don't pray to your Son with enough faith, hope, and love. So we ask you to pray for us. Our prayers are like bruised apples, which you polish and carry to his throne on a golden platter. You make them beautiful

for us, so that he is pleased to receive them.
Pray for us.

We are small and afraid of so many things,
so we seek the tender protection of your mother's heart. We need your help, most powerful
Virgin. Pray for us.

We fear to die alone, and we long for heaven. We dread the pangs of hell. Pray for us!
Holy Mary, Mother of God, pray for us sinners, now and at the hour of our death. Amen.

In dangers, in doubts, in difficulties, think of Mary,
call upon Mary. Let not her name depart from your
lips; never suffer it to leave your heart. And that you
may obtain the assistance of her prayer, neglect not
to walk in her footsteps. With her for [your] guide,
you shall never go astray; while invoking her, you
shall never lose heart; so long as she is in your mind,
you are safe from deception; while she holds your
hand, you cannot fall; under her protection you
have nothing to fear; if she walks before you, you
shall not grow weary; if she shows you favor, you
shall reach the goal.

Prayer

How often do we offer to do something for someone else? Today, offer your Hail Mary for someone
you've recently offered to help. Let it be a gift he
doesn't even know he needs.

Lisa Mladinich is the founder of AmazingCatechists.com, an author, and a speaker whose dynamic presentations on faith, catechetics, and women's issues can be heard at events around the country.

pray for *us* sinners

❦

Sarah Vabulas

The first thing that comes to mind when I hear the word *us* is community. How important community is in our lives!

Community can be a number of things: your family, a group of friends, or your church. At the core of our humanity, we all desire community. God knows this is in our hearts. No one wants to be alone. And this is reflected in so many aspects of our Catholic faith. A perfect example is in the Hail Mary when we ask Our Lady to pray for us.

That the Blessed Mother would be an advocate for us with her Son is an expression of her humility: Mary, one born without sin, who carried in her precious womb the baby Jesus, prays for us. As a woman, developing a relationship with the Blessed Mother has been one of the most fruitful experiences of my spiritual life.

Through Mary, we are all united in the saving grace of Jesus. Every person, every Catholic, falls into the *us* in this prayer. We all need grace, we all need prayer, and we all need forgiveness. Mary can advocate on our behalf for each of these things!

On a pilgrimage a few years ago, I traveled to Ephesus and was able to visit not only the ancient city but also the house of Mary where Mary lived with John before her Assumption. Here, prayers line a wall near the home. The faithful "tie on" a prayer to the wall and Mary takes the petition under her mantle. It was a beautiful experience and one I will carry with me forever. I looked upon the thousands of prayers on the wall and couldn't help but consider the community of believers that look to her as their Mother and ask for her care and protection.

In that moment, I felt united not only with the Blessed Mother but also with the thousands my prayer sat next to on the wall. United in a community of believers!

Holy Mary, pray for us!

Prayer

Whom are you praying with? Even if you're alone as you pray the Hail Mary today, you're surrounded—by angels and saints and perhaps even people. Let those who are with you, both seen and unseen, be part of your prayer in a special way.

Sarah Vabulas blogs at Catholic Drinkie *and is the author of* The Catholic Drinkie's Guide to Homebrewed Evangelism.

pray for us *sinners*

Donna-Marie Cooper O'Boyle

Sinners—now there's a powerful word. When we pray the Hail Mary we beseech our Mother in heaven to not merely *remember* us sinners but *pray* for us, too. It's a prayer of humility—we admit that we are sinners and we beg for prayers. And we ask this not just from anyone but from the Mother of God! We can't get any better than that except by asking God himself!

We know we can't get to heaven on our own merits and prayers. We absolutely need the intercession of the Mother of God. If we were more earnest about praying our Hail Marys and pondered them in our hearts as we prayed, we'd be enlightened to many graces and profound mysteries.

At what particular time are we begging in advance for Mary's powerful assistance? We specifically ask Mother Mary's prayers for *now* and *at the hour of our death*. We certainly need her prayers now while we're right in the thick of it, working out our salvation through the nitty-gritty details of daily life. Sometimes that *now* is rolling along and peachy, but many times that *now* is arduous and even painful. We absolutely need Mary, our Mother in heaven, to see us through— to actually lead us through the muck and grant us the graces we need to avoid the temptations and bombardments from our ungodly culture. We need Mary now more than ever.

We also need Mary at the hour of our death because we will be tempted by the devil to despair, and we will be weak, tired, and perhaps suffering immensely. Mary will help us lift our eyes and hearts to heaven. She, being so powerful over evil, will protect us sinners from the devil at the times we need protection most—now and at the hour of our death.

Let's not wait until the hour of our death to beseech our Mother Mary or just hope that she will run in to rescue us from the pits of hell at that time. Let's nurture a special friendship with her now so she can assist us in life and guide us safely to heaven.

Blessed Mother Teresa of Calcutta, whom I knew personally for about ten years, had a very close relationship with Mary and taught me a simple yet profound prayer that I pray often: "Mary, Mother of Jesus, be a Mother to me now." Mother Teresa stressed that Mother Mary wants to mother us sinners and wants us to call upon her often. She wants to be our Mother.

Mary, Mother of Jesus, be a Mother to me *now*!

Prayer

How do you need to be mothered? Turn to Mary today as you pray the Hail Mary and ask her to give you strength in the face of the sin in your life. Let her intercede for you and be an example of the path to Jesus.

Donna-Marie Cooper O'Boyle is an award-winning journalist, speaker, EWTN television host, and best-selling author of twenty books, including The Kiss of Jesus *and* The Miraculous Medal. *Find out more at DonnaCooperOBoyle.com.*

and at the hour of our death

Ellen Gable Hrkach

*N**ow* has always been one of my favorite words. Procrastinators don't like this word. As a wife, mother, NFP teacher, marriage preparation instructor, and writer with numerous deadlines, I live this word daily.

My mother also loved the word *now*. One of her commonly used expressions was "Now means now, not five minutes from now." Of course, if you ask my kids, they will tell you that I also use this expression more often than they would like. *Now* means "without further delay." Now I must change my baby's diaper or his bottom will get a painful rash. Now I must feed my children or they will go hungry and become ill. Now I must finish this post so I can move on to the next deadline.

The Hail Mary is a beautiful and powerful prayer. In the first part, we recite the words of the archangel Gabriel and then those of Elizabeth. In the second part, we ask Mary to pray for us. And to pray for us *now*.

Mary said yes to God immediately (without delay). She didn't say, "Maybe later." She said, "May it be done to me according to your word" (Lk 1:38). Mary nurtured and protected the unborn, then newborn, then child Jesus. She watched her Son suffer in agony and die a barbaric death and held his brutalized body in her arms after death. She knows intimately what it is like to watch a loved one suffer and die.

"Now and at the hour of our death." Nineteen years ago, I had occasion to pray these words with desperation as I drifted in and out of consciousness in the back of an ambulance. I was weak, scared, and in excruciating pain, the result of a tumor that was rapidly growing inside my abdomen and causing massive internal bleeding. At the time, I was the young mother of three small boys: ten months, three, and five years of age. I was afraid of dying but, more importantly, I didn't want my little boys growing up without a mother.

"Now and at the hour of our death." I prayed these words with such fervency because I realized that it might very well be the hour of my death.

In the back of that ambulance, the moment I prayed those words, I no longer felt afraid; I no longer felt concerned for my boys. It was as if all the worry and fear were stripped away and an all-encompassing peace permeated every cell, every artery, every muscle in my body. Most importantly, this peace filled and comforted my troubled soul. I sensed a presence around me, almost cradling me. It happened so quickly that it took me by surprise.

Obviously, I did not die that day. But I caught a glimpse of death and a glimmer of heaven. I asked for help *now* because I needed it immediately. Jesus and his Blessed Mother were (and are) dependable and work quickly.

Now is a good time to take stock in our spiritual life. Now is a good time to take care of our bodies, our minds, and, most importantly, our souls. And I know, without a doubt, that when it is my time to return home to heaven, Mary will be there with me, at that exact moment, praying that her Son gives me the all-encompassing grace I need for the journey home.

Prayer

What are you waiting for? Pray your Hail Mary *now*. And pray it when the now of the moment strikes you, because the present moment is a powerful way to stay in touch with God.

Ellen Gable Hrkach is president of the Catholic Writers Guild as well as a publisher, editor, and author of five books. Find out more at EllenGable.com.

now *and* at the hour
of our death

Peggy Bowes

Ikneel in front of the plaster statue of Mary after Mass, frustrated that my relationship with my heavenly Mother is somehow statue-like: an attempt at trying to capture something beautiful but not quite getting there.

Occasionally there are moments when it's just right, like during my first pregnancy when I felt as if Mary held me gently in her arms as I fought through waves of nausea, assuring me that becoming a mother was the greatest thing I could ever do.

Then there was the time when my Little Flowers Girls' Club May crowning ceremony was not as perfect as I'd hoped, and I felt as if I'd somehow disappointed her. As I silently begged forgiveness, I was overcome by the most wonderful sense of love and the realization that the little girls I had guided were indeed honoring her in a way that pleased her immensely. It's in those rare moments of grace that I truly feel the *and* between Mary and me. Yet most of the time it is elusive, like the plaster statue that will always be an unworthy imitation.

In an attempt to strengthen my relationship with Mary, I recently made the Total Consecration to Jesus through Mary, using St. Louis de Montfort's thirty-three-day program. It was one of the most difficult periods of my life, and I believed that the trial would somehow result in an almost magical transformation of my life and my devotion to Mary. It didn't. In fact, she seemed more distant than ever.

I reflected on those moments of grace when I felt truly united with Mary and realized they occurred when I gave her my whole heart without reserve. Of course! I felt close to Mary when I imitated her and her complete giving of self to God. When I didn't, I was the plaster statue, the unworthy imitation.

St. Louis de Montfort understood this perfectly. In *True Devotion to the Blessed Virgin*, he says, "Beg her to lend you her heart, saying, 'O Mary, I take you for my all; give me your heart.'"

So there it is. If I want to strengthen the *and* between Mary and me, I must borrow her heart and give her my all, becoming a worthy imitation, not a dim shadow of a plaster statue.

Prayer

Imitating Mary can seem an imposing and impossible task. Don't let it scare you or keep you from trying! As you pray the Hail Mary today, ask for the *and* between you and Mary to strengthen so that you can become more like her in all the ways God intends.

Peggy Bowes, an Air Force Academy graduate, former flight instructor, and personal trainer, is very devoted to the Blessed Mother and her favorite prayer, the Rosary. Find out more at RosaryWorkout.com.

now and *at* the hour
of our death

Daria Sockey

At the hour of our death. *At* is defined as a preposition used to indicate a point or a place occupied in space or in time.

Oh, how I want the Mother of Jesus to "occupy" the hour of my death. To use what may be a silly example, think of the Occupy Wall Street movement. These people—whatever we may think of their politics—take over a city park and set up camp there. They don't leave. They are there for the duration of the scheduled protest.

That's how I want Our Lady to be present in prayer *at* the hour of my death. I'm begging her to occupy that moment in time, staying there for the duration. Pitching her tent by my deathbed and not leaving until it is over—seeing me through to the end. Then, and only then, she can leave, taking me with her.

Prayer

Death isn't something comfortable to think about or ponder, and yet we must. Whether we want it to be or not, death is inevitable. As you pray your Hail Mary today, remember those who are close to death and ask for the grace to hold Mary's hand when you face death—your own or a loved one's.

Daria Sockey, a mother of seven living in western Pennsylvania, is the author of The Everyday Catholic's Guide to the Liturgy of the Hours. *Find out more at her blog,* Coffee and Canticles.

now and at the hour
of our death

Susie Lloyd

I think about *the* hour of my death every single day.

Most people who meet me or who know me through my humor books think I've got a sanguine temperament. If you're not up on temperament terminology, this is Tigger—happy-go-lucky party animal who tends to leap upon people and knock them down. Just imagine this conversation between Tigger and Pooh:

> Tigger: *I recognize you. You're the one that's stuffed with fluff.*
> Pooh: *Yeah. And you're sitting on it.*
> Tigger: *Yeah. And it's comfy too!*

But did you know that most comics are melancholic? Not, however, like Eeyore: *Nobody cares. . . .*

More like Rabbit: *Why did I ever invite that bear to lunch? Why, oh, why, oh, why?* Able to see all the little details that make up the big picture. And fret about them.

Well, is there a bigger picture than our salvation, and is there a more important detail than *the* hour of our death?

The hour of our death is not an isolated hour. It depends on all the other hours of our life. Not to say that we should fret and worry over our past sins, though these details seem so richly to deserve it. The devil may be in the details, but God's in the big picture.

I used to spend a fair bit of time worrying over my past sins. So on retreat once I made a General Confession. This is an exercise where you repeat all your big, ugly sins even though you've confessed them already, for the purpose of . . . I'm not really sure. Maybe because that's what you do on a retreat? Anyway, for a solid half hour at least, I recited a tearful and humiliating list of my sins to an ancient missionary Jesuit. He listened kindly and patiently, and when I was through (through a box of tissues, that is) he finally spoke up.

"Thank God," he said slowly, "that through all of that you never lost your faith."

The big picture.

After that I have been developing a more positive relationship with *the* hour of my own death.

My kids are jealous. I try to include them but they resist. When our choir learns an exquisite new Palestrina piece, I turn to them and say, "Please sing this at my funeral." When we visit the cemeteries where my mom or mother-in-law are buried, I remind them that I want the kind of tombstone you can sit on so they can get comfortable and stay awhile.

The way I think about my mother's death twenty-one years ago has changed, too. For years I felt like I was a train going in a straight line and she was left on the platform. Every day took me, against my will, further and further away from her. Now that my life is very likely at least half over, I feel as if the train has rounded a bend and every day brings me closer and closer to her.

"Mom's being morbid again!"

Not at all. Nothing I say will make it come any sooner. Nor delay it—no, not even by an hour. Here and now is here and now. I love my life, and I will be here for them as long as God permits (though can someone up there tell him that I really don't want to look old?).

Meanwhile, can I help it if I think of heaven? I have a fantasy that someday we will all stand around and compare death stories the way we now compare birth stories.

"Can you believe it? I had just put the deposit on our new house. How about you?"

"I was flayed alive."

"You win."

Don't get me wrong. I dread *the* hour of my death. For one thing, I'm no angel, and for another,

I can't think of an easy way to handle it. As my mother-in-law would say, "I'm a devout coward."

But there is a part of me that looks forward to . . . something.

That mysterious hidden something outside of time or anything I've experienced and yet . . . fully human. A moment. And in that moment I am with my mother again and I am introducing her to her grandchildren. And there is no more fear. No more dread. No more *Why, oh, why, oh, why?*

There is an hour. It is my hour. It is *the* hour.

I pray to Mary, my Mother in heaven, to be with me during that hour and during all the hours on which that hour depends.

Prayer

What moment are you living today? How can Mary be part of it and guide you closer to Jesus in the midst of the day you're having, the challenges you're facing, the life you're leading? Pray the Hail Mary, asking Mary to be with you.

Susie Lloyd is the author of Please Don't Drink the Holy Water; Bless Me, Father, for I Have Kids; *and* Yes, God! *She has also written many articles. Find out more at SusieLloyd.com.*

now and at the *hour* of our death

Karen Edmisten

An hour. Depending on your point of view, it is a blink or an eternity.

Consider a mom. An hour falls on the blink side of the fence: "I have one hour to finish (insert forty-eight projects) before I have to pick up the kids from (insert thirty-seven activities)."

But for a child an hour lands—nay, *thuds*—firmly in the territory of eternity: "I have to wait an *ow-errrrr* before it's time to leave for the water park?!"

For our Blessed Mother, though, it's all the same. It's a moment. *The* moment. "The hour of our death." And we ask her to pray for us in that moment.

The hour of my death refers to the precise moment at which I'll pass from this life to the next. Perhaps that will feel like a flash to me, though I doubt it, as that's what I imagine the hour holds for those

saints who will zoom past "Go" and collect the ultimate two hundred dollars.

No, for me, I am guessing my hour—my slog
toward heaven—might feel like that child's per-
ception of the It-Cannot-Arrive-Soon-Enough-
Water-Park. I'm imagining a best-case scenario
here: I made a good confession right before I died,
so at least there's no mortal sin mucking things up,
but I've still got purgatory to wade through, and it's
gonna take a while.

I sometimes imagine the lobby of purgatory as a
giant movie theater in which I am forced to sit in a
horribly scratchy, lumpy chair. Of course I'm wear-
ing shorts too, so I feel every coarse, wooly thread
as I fidget in my seat, trying to get comfortable.
And did I mention that the shorts are ill-fitting? The
waistband cuts, but there's nothing to do about that
until the movie is over. It's way too hot, and there's
no restroom in this theater either. Obviously there's
no popcorn, and the only thing to drink is a wa-
tered-down Dr Pepper (I hate Dr Pepper). The fea-
ture film is a wretched excuse for entertainment—
it's all my unfinished business, the temporal messes
I left behind, the things for which I haven't atoned,
illustrations of the sins to which I'm still attached.
I'm squirming. I can't *wait* for this movie to end because clearly I've still got a huge cleansing coming
my way. This is just the purgatorial equivalent of
running the bath water.

It's ironic that on this side of heaven children perceive time as something that crawls, while we adults are convinced it flies. At the hour of my death, I'm certain I'll rediscover that an hour can indeed crawl, seemingly forever, as I work through the consequences of my life choices. And yet an innocent child, who can't bear to wait that "ow-errrrr" for anything of import, will find herself in the presence of Jesus in an instant.

An hour is what we make of it. My blink, my child's eternity—they are the same in the eyes of the Lord, who stands outside of time.

Mary, beautiful, gracious, ever-present Blessed Mother, pray for me to make use of every minute, to stretch every bit of time taken for granted, to turn around every bit of impatience, to live for Jesus *every hour* so that your prayers for me, now and at the hour of my death, will not be for nothing.

Prayer

Can you give Mary an hour today? Maybe it will be in ten-minute chunks, or maybe it will be all at once. Consider how you can give her an hour, and pray the Hail Mary that she will help you make it happen.

Karen Edmisten, a former atheist, is the author of Deathbed Conversions, After Miscarriage, Through the Year with Mary, *and* The Rosary. *Find out more at KarenEdmisten.com.*

now and at the hour
of our death

Shelly Henley Kelly

For such a small two-letter word, each use within this prayer has carried a different, though very powerful, meaning.

Full *of* grace
Fruit *of* thy womb
Mother *of* God
Hour *of* our death

In this instance, we are looking at *of* being used to indicate a position in the time of an action. *Of* in this moment of the prayer indicates not just any action or occurrence but our final breaths of life—our imperfect, admittedly sinful, life. Also important is the preceding word, *hour*, denoting not just any brief moment but a specific period of time. For no one knows when her moment of death will arrive, only that it will come.

We implore Mary, who stood at the foot of the cross witnessing her Son's death, to be our Mother, remembering us in her prayers and guiding us in our final hour that we may be worthy of the promises of Christ. Even the *Catechism* reminds us that it is not enough to "give ourselves over to her now, in the Today of our lives" (CCC 2677) but that we should also do so in the hour of our death.

Just as she delivered our Lord to us, we pray for her to deliver us to her Son, our Lord. In each prayer, we invite her not only to pray for us now but also to herald us on our journey to being received into the presence of God.

Prayer

What is your cross? What is the view as you look up at it? How does it weigh on you right now? Pray the Hail Mary and ask for the grace to perform the action—or inaction—that's needed today.

Shelly Henley Kelly, a frenetic working mother of three, is fanning into flame the gift God gave her via the blog Of Sound Mind and Spirit, *shared with her sister, Lisa Jones.*

now and at the hour
of *our* death

Cat Hodge

Death seems like the ultimate isolation. Everyone knows "you can't take it with you." At the moment of death, a person leaves behind everything earthly and familiar: his possessions, his family, even his body. The image of standing naked and alone before the seat of judgment is so terrifying that humans have long sought ways to avoid death, to put off that moment in which one is alone with every sin exposed.

The paradox is that this ultimately isolating experience is the one inevitable thing shared by every member of the human race. "Pray for us sinners, now and at the hour of our death." *Our* death, because everyone must die. *Our* death, because Mary also has died. We beg her prayers for those who are dying, as others in turn pray for us, and this densely woven blanket of prayer covers our nakedness before the throne of God. In the end, the moment of death is not a moment of isolation, because the prayers of both the living and the dead converge on this critical point in time in which the final temporal choice must be made.

And in that hour of death, Mary, as requested again and again in her own prayer, accompanies every sinner before the seat of judgment, even those who have never known to turn to her. Her maternal sense draws her to intercede for all souls, never leaving them alone and unprotected. She lavishes the same love and attention on each dying person as she did on her dying Son, joining that soul to Jesus' at the moment of his death, so that "our death" becomes a literal expression of communion with God.

And the more frequently we pray the Hail Mary, the more likely it becomes that death will not be leaving the familiar world but stepping into it for the first time, accompanied by those whose deaths are united to ours through our mutual prayers.

Prayer

Today, let your one Hail Mary multiply into more. How? Maybe there's a small act of service you can provide to someone who needs it. Perhaps there's a person who needs your presence in a special way. How about that pull you feel in your heart? Let the fruit of your prayer lead you to wherever God wants you to be today and what he wants you to do.

Cat Hodge blogs with her husband, Brendan, and homeschools her six kids in a grand old house in Delaware, Ohio, where she also writes novels as a hobby. Find out more at DarwinCatholic.blogspot.com.

now and at the hour
of our *death*

Paula Huston

I t seems I have reached the dying age.

Not that I myself am facing imminent death, or at least, not to the best of my knowledge. But a whole generation, the generation that gave birth to mine, is rapidly going the way of all flesh, and these days, I am finding myself on the front lines in this losing battle against nature.

A few years ago, it was my petite and elegant mother-in-law, reduced, at the end, to a child-sized wraith in a white nightgown. Then it was Fr. Bernard, my first confessor and monk friend, who succumbed to Parkinson's a day after our last visit.

Right now I am helping Margaret Joy, who has never smoked, navigate the final stages of lung cancer. During my weekly visits, I read to her from C. S. Lewis. Meanwhile, my stalwart father-in-law, a ninety-year-old World War II veteran, has begun sleeping up to eighteen hours at a time, a sure sign, says the hospice nurse, that he is "dwindling."

I remember when my own mother went through this time of life: the loss of both her parents within a few years of one another, and the strange sense that at sixty years old, she'd become an orphan. Yet compared to the disorienting grief she experienced when one of her grandchildren was killed, the sadness of losing her parents felt like indulgence in sentimentality.

But it shouldn't have. The human problem with death is age-irrelevant: as the poet John Donne says, "Any man's death diminishes me." Since we are made in the image of God, our purpose in life is to love. We spend our years weaving relationships, webs of silken thread that unite our souls to the souls of others. When these threads are snapped in death, we lose not only a person but, at least for a while, our conviction that the effort we've put into loving and living means anything at all. Death cannot help but bring doubt.

And so I am grateful for the final words of the Hail Mary: "Holy Mary, Mother of God, pray for us sinners, now and at the hour of our death." In Mary, we claim the parent who will never leave us orphans, who will comfort us when we are bereaved, who will intercede for us when we are too shaken by despairing grief to ask for what we need, and who will strengthen and sustain us when, tremulous and uncertain, we ourselves arrive at the great portal to the next world.

None of us escapes death, neither the death of those we love nor our own. The irony is that no matter how we abhor it, how it offends at the most primitive level of our being, we must go through it if we are ever to meet God face-to-face. To enter the future, we must relinquish the present. Here is where Mary can be of such help—the mother who stands close by as, like trusting little children, we fling ourselves forward into mystery.

Prayer

Are you afraid of death? If so, you're not alone. As you pray the Hail Mary today, let your heart be at peace in the face of the death all around us, the death that is inevitable in our lives, the death that will undoubtedly cause us pain. Let Mary hold you and let the prayer be a lifeline to God's comfort.

Camaldolese Benedictine oblate Paula Huston teaches in the Seattle Pacific University Master of Fine Arts program and is the author of two novels and six books of spiritual nonfiction, including the forthcoming One Ordinary Sunday: A Meditation on the Mystery of the Mass.

Amen

Fr. Patrick Toner

A men is from the Hebrew root *amam*, meaning "to believe or to be faithful." It means more than just an intellectual accent to a doctrine or statement. It is a promise to be bound to act upon the words you have just affirmed. We often hear the word translated as "So be it."

For Jews, there was no distinction between hearing a word and doing what was heard. The word *shema* meant "to hear and obey." Amen is applied to confirmation or an endorsement of what God says. It can be used to express hope or to confirm a blessing, a prayer, a curse, or an oath.

Amen is much more than an ending to a prayer. When another leads the prayer, it is our affirmation of what was prayed. The Church teaches *lex orandi lex credendi*, or "what you pray is what you believe." The Amen at the end of any prayer is like signing your name to the Declaration of Independence: you've put your life on the line. Live all of your Amens.

Prayer

This is not the end of our prayer but rather the beginning of a new journey. Stake your life on what the Hail Mary says and stands for. Pray it today with a new conviction and the commitment to continue praying it every day.

Fr. Patrick Toner, a priest of forty years in the Diocese of Columbus, Ohio, has served as a pastor, military chaplain, prison chaplain, spiritual director, and editorialist.

Conclusion

Once upon a time, I thought I was supposed to write a Marian book. I was gung ho. I was all set. I had it all planned out.

And it completely fizzled.

A few years later, a book project came my way that involved the Blessed Mother, and I thought, "Ah, here is the Marian book! I was just off on topic and timing!"

And then, a few short months ago, the folks at Ave Maria Press approached me about compiling a series of blog posts into a devotional. They were blog posts that examined the Hail Mary word by word. It was, without a doubt, a Marian book. It is, in fact, the book you hold in your hands or on your e-reader.

But is it *the* Marian book? Honestly, I don't know.

This is how it always is with me and Mary. I'm the little girl who has everything figured out. I have things all organized and I'm telling her just how it will be. I bring her flowers and gifts and treasures that I think are the best gifts *ever*. She's gracious and loving, taking them all and smiling at me.

Later, I look on to see that the flowers were wilted dandelions, the gifts were scrappy and dented, and the treasures could be better categorized as junk. Why didn't she say something?

Mary's always guiding me, always leading me, always directing my steps, but she's polite about it. She lets me meander along and make mistakes, even make a fool of myself. She knows me well enough to know that tugging on my arm will only result in a pulling war; I won't follow along and cooperate, no matter what. She doesn't yell at me or badger me or nag me. Instead, she stays around, loving me unconditionally. It's her presence more than anything that wins me over.

When I became Catholic in 2001, I marveled that I was doing so. When I got married in 2003, I smiled inwardly that I was giving in to what I had long considered an outdated institution. When I had my first child in 2005—and with each subsequent child—I was astounded at the work involved and the joy inherent in my role.

I never thought I'd be a wife and a mom; I never thought I'd be a writer. They just weren't ever on my radar. They didn't matter to me—or I didn't think they did. And yet, here I am, years later, using all those words (and quite a few others) to describe myself.

I credit the intercession of the Blessed Mother for the small, invisible-to-all-other-eyes miracles that have been worked within me. Because that's what conversion truly is: a series of small interior miracles. I'm very much a work in progress. My rough edges may never be smoothed, but they'll be different than they are now.

Going through the Hail Mary as we just have, slowly and deliberately, considering and pondering, isn't natural for me. I'm all about crossing things off my list, accomplishing the next task, getting to the end. And yet, we need the space and the silence that come from this sort of approach. We need to give ourselves the gift of time with Jesus, and few people can show us how to do that better than Mary herself.

It's my prayer that you'll revisit the Hail Mary again soon, slowly and one word at a time. Maybe you'll even consider writing your own reflections about the words that speak to you as you pray it.

This isn't a passing fad or a one-time exercise. This is a change of mind. May we look for ways to grow closer to Jesus through Mary, especially in our prayer and conversations with God.

Appendix: Titles for Mary

Deacon Tom Fox

Here is a nonexhaustive list, which I offer to you for meditation. Perhaps you'd be willing to pick a few each day and then contemplate and pray about Mary under one of her unique and honorary titles.

Adam's Deliverance
Advocate of Eve
Advocate of Sinners
All Chaste
All Fair and Immaculate
All Good
Aqueduct of Grace
Archetype of Purity and
  Innocence
Ark Gilded by the Holy Spirit
Ark of the Covenant
Assumed into Heaven
Basilica of Saint Mary Major
Blessed among Women
Blessed Virgin Mary
Bridal Chamber of the Lord
Bride of Christ
Bride of Heaven
Bride of the Canticle
Bride of the Father
Bride Unwed
Cause of Our Joy
Chosen before the Ages

Comfort of Christians
Comforter of the Afflicted
Conceived without Original Sin
Consoler of the Afflicted
Court of the Eternal King
Created Temple of the Creator
Crown of Virginity
Daughter of Men
David's Daughter
Deliverer from All Wrath
Deliverer of Christian Nations
Destroyer of Heresies
Dispenser of Grace
Dwelling Place for God
Dwelling Place of the Spirit
Earth Unsown
Earth Untouched and Virginal
Eastern Gate
Espousal of the Virgin Mary
Ever Green and Fruitful
Ever Virgin
Eve's Tears Redeeming
Exalted above the Angels

Expectation of the Blessed Virgin
  Mary
Flower of Carmel
Flower of Jesse's Root
Formed without Sin
Fountain of Living Water
Free from Every Stain
Full of Grace
Garden Enclosed
Gate of Heaven
God's Eden
God's Olive Tree
God's Vessel
Handmaiden of the Lord
Healing Balm of Integrity
Health of the Sick
Helper of All in Danger
Holy in Soul and Body
Holy Mountain of Our Lady
Holy Protection of the Mother
  of God
Hope of Christians
House Built by Wisdom
House of Gold
Immaculate Conception
Immaculate Heart
Immaculate Heart of Mary
Immaculate Mother
Immaculate Virgin
Incorruptible Wood of the Ark
Inviolate One
Joseph's Spouse
King's Mother
Lady Most Chaste
Lady Most Venerable
Lady of Good Help
Lady of Grace
Lady of Mercy
Lady of Peace
Lady of Perpetual Help
Lady of Sorrows
Lady of the Rosary

Lady of Victory
Lamp Unquenchable
Life-Giver to Posterity
Light Cloud of Heavenly Rain
Lily among Thorns
Living Temple of the Deity
Loom of the Incarnation
Madonna of Miracles
Madonna of St. Luke
Marketplace for Salutary
  Exchange
Mary of the Assumptions
Mary of the Hurons
Mary the Blessed Virgin
Mary, Blessed Virgin
Mary, Help of Christians
Mary, Mediatrix of All Graces
Mary, Mother of God
Mary, Queen of Africa
Mary, Queen of Angels
Mary, Queen of Peace
Mary, Star of the Sea
Mary, Virgin Mother of Grace
Mary's Immaculate Conception
Mater Dei
Maternity of the Blessed Virgin
  Mary
Mediatrix
Mediatrix of All Graces
Mediatrix of Salvation
Mediatrix of the Mediator
Minister of Life
Mirror of Justice
More Beautiful Than Beauty
More Glorious Than Paradise
More Gracious Than Grace
More Holy Than the Cherubim,
  the Seraphim, and the Entire
  Angelic Hosts
Morning Star
Most Holy Name of Mary
Most Humble

Most Venerable
Mother and Virgin
Mother Inviolate
Mother Most Admirable
Mother Most Amiable
Mother Most Chaste
Mother Most Pure
Mother of Christians
Mother of Christ's Members
Mother of Divine Grace
Mother of God
Mother of Good Counsel
Mother of Jesus Christ
Mother of Men
Mother of Our Creator
Mother of Our Head
Mother of Our Savior
Mother of the Church
Mother of the Mystical Body
Mother of Wisdom
Mother Undefiled My Body's
    Healing
My Soul's Saving
Mystical Rose
Nature's Re-creation
Nature's Restoration
Neck of the Mystical Body
Never Fading Wood
New Eve
Notre Dame of Chartres
Notre Dame of Easton
Notre Dame of Paris
Nourisher of God and Man
Olive Tree of the Father's
    Compassion
Only Bridge of God to Men
Our Immaculate Queen
Our Lady in America
Our Lady Mediatrix of All Grace
Our Lady of Africa
Our Lady of Arabia
Our Lady of Bethlehem

Our Lady of Calvary
Our Lady of Charity
Our Lady of Consolation
Our Lady of Częstochowa
Our Lady of Europe
Our Lady of Fatima
Our Lady of Good Counsel
Our Lady of Good Help
Our Lady of Grace
Our Lady of Guadalupe
Our Lady of High Grace
Our Lady of Hungary
Our Lady of Japan
Our Lady of Knock
Our Lady of La Leche
Our Lady of LaSallette
Our Lady of Lebanon
Our Lady of Limerick
Our Lady of Loretto
Our Lady of Lourdes
Our Lady of Mercy
Our Lady of Miracles
Our Lady of Montserrat
Our Lady of Mount Carmel
Our Lady of Nazareth
Our Lady of Peace
Our Lady of Perpetual Help
Our Lady of Pilar
Our Lady of Pompeii
Our Lady of Prompt Succor
Our Lady of Providence
Our Lady of Ransom
Our Lady of Safe Travel
Our Lady of Sorrows
Our Lady of St. Luke
Our Lady of Tears
Our Lady of the Americas
Our Lady of the Angels
Our Lady of the Assumption
Our Lady of the Cape
Our Lady of the Conquest

Our Lady of the Flight into
Egypt
Our Lady of the Golden Heart
Our Lady of the Gulf
Our Lady of the Hermits
Our Lady of the Highways
Our Lady of the Holy Letter
Our Lady of the Holy Rosary
Our Lady of the Holy Souls
Our Lady of the Immaculate
Conception
Our Lady of the Incarnation
Our Lady of the Kodiak and the
Islands
Our Lady of the Milk and Happy Delivery
Our Lady of the Miraculous
Medal
Our Lady of the Most Blessed
Sacrament
Our Lady of the Most Holy
Rosary
Our Lady of the Pillar of
Saragossa
Our Lady of the Pines
Our Lady of the Prairie
Our Lady of the Presentation
Our Lady of the Rosary
Our Lady of the Snow
Our Lady of the Snows
Our Lady of the Thorns
Our Lady of the Valley
Our Lady of the Wayside
Our Lady of the Woods
Our Lady of Victories
Our Lady of Victory
Our Lady of Washington
Our Lady Who Appeared
Our Lady, Cause of Our Joy
Our Lady, Gate of Heaven
Our Lady, Help of Christians
Our Lady, Mother of the Church

Our Lady, Queen of All Saints
Our Lady, Queen of the Apostles
Our Lady, Refuge of Sinners
Our Own Sweet Mother
Paradise Fenced against the
Serpent
Paradise of Innocence and
Immortality
Paradise of the Second Adam
Paradise Planted by God
Patronage of Our Lady
Patroness and Protectress
Perfume of Faith
Presentation of Mary at the
Temple
Preserved from All Sin
Protectress from All Hurt
Purification of Mary
Purity of the Blessed Virgin
Mary
Queen of All Saints
Queen of Angels
Queen of Creation
Queen of Heaven
Queen of Heaven and Earth
Queen of Martyrs
Queen of Nigeria
Queen of Peace
Queen Unconquered
Queenship of Mary
Refuge in Time of Danger
Refuge of Sinners
Rich in Mercy
Rose Ever Blooming
Salve Regina
Sanctuary of the Holy Spirit
Scepter of Orthodoxy
Seat of Wisdom
Second Eve
Singular Vessel of Devotion
Sister and Mother
Source of Virginity

Spiritual Vessel
Spotless Dove of Beauty
Star of the Sea
Star That Bore the Sea
Supplant for Sinners
Surpassing Eden's Gardens
Surpassing the Heavens
Surpassing the Seraphim
Sweet Flowering and Gracious
  Mercy
Tabernacle of God
Tabernacle of the Word
Temple Divine
Temple Indestructible
Temple of the Lord's Body
Theotokos
Throne of the King
Tower of David
Tower of Ivory
Tower Unassailable
Treasure House of Life
Treasure of Immortality
Treasure of the World Undefiled
Undefiled Treasure of Virginity
Un-Dug Well of Remission's
  Waters
Unlearned in the Ways of Eve
Unplowed Field of Heaven's
  Bread
Unwatered Vineyard of Immor-
  tality's Wine
Vessel of Honor
Victor over the Serpent
Virgin by the Sea
Virgin Inviolate
Virgin Most Faithful
Virgin Most Merciful
Virgin Most Powerful
Virgin Most Prudent
Virgin Most Pure
Virgin Mothe
Virgin of Charity

Virgin of Virgins
Visitation of the Blessed
  Virgin Mary
Wedded to God
Woman Clothed with the Sun
Workshop of the Incarnatio

Sarah A. Reinhard is a Catholic author, blogger, speaker, and freelance writer. She contributes regularly to the *National Catholic Register*, *CatholicMom.com*, *Integrated Catholic Life*, *Catholic Exchange*, and *SpiritualDirection.com*.

Reinhard is the author of a number of books and writes a monthly column in the Diocese of Columbus's *The Catholic Times*. She earned a master's degree in marketing and communications from Franklin University and has worked for many years for corporate and nonprofit organizations. She lives in central Ohio with her husband and four children.